THE ANSWER TRAP

Why we stop thinking
when it matters most and
how to break free

KATE CHRISTIANSEN

HANDSON
MEDIA

Published by Handson Media, Melbourne. enquiries@handsonmedia.com.au

A catalogue record for this work is available from the National Library of Australia

NATIONAL LIBRARY OF AUSTRALIA

The Answer Trap: Why we stop thinking when it matters most and how to break free.

Written by Kate Christiansen

ISBN: 978-0-9944751-4-5

The Answer Trap™ contents, definition, concepts, formats and graphic representations are trademarks of 100% Care Pty Ltd.

Cover design – Concept design and drafting by Kate Christiansen, final digital production by DALL-E and Hammad Publishing.

Internal illustrations and diagrams - Concept design and drafting by Kate Christiansen, digital production by DALL-E and Zel Petisme Uy

Editor - Gabrielle Prior

ADVANCED PRAISE FOR THE ANSWER TRAP

'**Every leader must read this!** The concepts in the book are clearly articulated and resonate strongly, and Kate's compelling storytelling brings them to life. **I found myself screaming out 'Yes, help!'** as she captured, with stunning accuracy, how we habitually respond to problems: favouring speed, decisiveness and closure over thoughtful engagement, purpose and alignment. **This book doesn't just explain the trap we fall into. It helps you get out of it.** Kate outlines practical, accessible steps to help break the cycle and re-set—without ever oversimplifying. The structure and simplicity of the writing meant the ideas landed clearly. I've already started using them consciously in both my personal and professional life.'

Trish Mikhael, Chief Financial Officer

'**Under pressure, our brain reaches for relief, not clarity, and AI only speeds that up.** *The Answer Trap* offers a powerful antidote: a clear, practical method to interrupt default thinking and engage with complexity on purpose. Whether you're navigating complex decisions personally or leading others through uncertainty, this book helps you reclaim the one thing AI can't replicate… deliberate human thinking.'

Andy McKechnie, Former Banking Executive and Board Advisor

'**At a time when we risk outsourcing our thinking to AI, this book is a timely reminder that discomfort isn't something to avoid.** It's easy to forget that we grow when we're outside our comfort zone. *The Answer Trap* gives practical tools to pause, build alignment around the right question, and avoid the trap of making quick or easy decisions - whether that's through AI or just default thinking.'

Angela Skandarajah, Board Chair

'**A must-read for any leader who wants to have impact in this fast-evolving world.** This book is a much-needed permission slip to slow down, recalibrate and lead with greater intention. I deeply related to the stories and the messy, everyday traps leaders fall into. The book normalises how common these thinking patterns are and shows that there's a way out if you can recognise your defaults early enough. The frameworks and questioning techniques are grounded in real self-awareness and remind us that it's not speed, but clarity - rooted in emotion, aspiration and reflection - that drives meaningful progress.'

Caroline Monzon, GM – People and Culture

'**I could really identify with this.** Every leader comes up against these issues, and this book gives you the tools to deal with them.'

Gary Allen, CEO

'**When I first read the abstract for The Answer Trap, I immediately thought, 'This is the book I need right now!', and I was not wrong.** Too often in our busy lives it is much easier to respond with a quick answer and move on to the next task, even though we know that we shouldn't. Kate really understands how many of us operate and feel in those moments of pressure and has provided some real-life solutions on how we can move beyond the 'quick response' to thinking about the 'right response'. I may not succeed in changing my patterns all the time but I will definitely be on the look-out for those critical moments where I can change my thinking'

Karma Auden, Chief Financial Officer

'**This book brings humanity back to how we think.** It highlights the risk of taking easy answers and offers a practical, intentional path to escape *The Answer Trap*. The Moment Method, especially the shift from individual reflection to cultivating a culture that thinks together—feels both timely and timeless. This book doesn't just offer insight, it offers a way forward.'

Brett Comer, Chief Finance & Operating Officer

'**This book is a powerful guide for anyone navigating change, complexity and the urge to pretend they're sure.** It gave me practical insights I could immediately connect to real scenarios I'm facing—especially the idea of catching the moment before it catches you. The distinction between agreement and alignment shifted how I think about leading through pressure.'

Melinda Benbow, Supply Planning Manager

ACKNOWLEDGEMENT

No book is written alone. This one was shaped through countless conversations, challenges and generous acts of thinking together.

To everyone who shared their time, their questions and their perspectives – thank you. Special thanks to the early readers and pioneering thinkers who pushed the ideas further. Your feedback made this book better.

And to the friends and family who kept cheering from the sidelines: you helped me keep going. You know who you are.

ABOUT THE AUTHOR

Kate Christiansen is an award-winning author, sought-after speaker and advisor who helps people create clarity when the stakes are high and the path ahead isn't clear.

With a background in executive leadership, transformation and consulting, Kate has spent decades inside fast-changing environments, working with leaders, teams and systems under pressure. She's known for helping people spot the exact moment their thinking gets stuck - and giving them the tools to move forward with purpose.

From multi-billion dollar mergers to moments of team-level ambiguity, Kate brings real-world insight to the challenge of leading in complexity. Her work is grounded in lived experience and sharpened through decades of practice.

The Answer Trap is her third book. It builds on the foundations of *The Thrive Cycle* (on adaptive capability) and *Curly Conversations for Teams* (on shared thinking), but goes deeper, into the moment where thinking breaks down, and how we can reclaim it before we default to fast answers.

Kate lives in Melbourne, Australia, and works globally with change-makers and system shapers to build cultures that think differently—especially when it matters most.

Learn more at: **www.katechristiansen.com.au**

CONTENTS

INTRODUCTION: THE BOOK I DIDN'T WRITE   8

PART 1: CATCH THE TRAP   17

1. THE RIP   19
2. WHY THE ANSWER FEELS SO RIGHT, EVEN IF IT'S WRONG   36
3. THE REAL COST   46
4. THE AI CHALLENGE   63
5. BEYOND THE ANSWERS   76

PART 2: MAKE THE SWITCH   91

6. THE THINKING PROBLEM   94
7. WHAT FIRES FIRST?   101
8. EVERYDAY THINKING   110
9. WHEN YOUR AUTOPILOT TAKES OVER   123
10. THE DRIFT INTO DEFAULT   140

PART 3: MASTER YOUR MOMENT   155

11. THE MOMENT METHOD   158
12. ACTIVATE   174
13. ARTICULATE   197
14. NAVIGATE   222

PART 4: IGNITE GROUP MOMENTUM   241

15. WHY SMART GROUPS GET STUCK   244
16. ACCELERATE   253
17. CULTIVATE   268

PART 5: THE HUMAN IMPERATIVE   289

18. YOUR MIND. YOUR MOMENT.   290

AN INVITATION   302
FURTHER READING AND REFERENCES   304

INTRODUCTION:
THE BOOK I DIDN'T WRITE

I pressed enter.

What appeared on the screen amazed me. The language was sharp, the structure clear, the ideas neatly packaged. Generative AI had answered my simple question with speed and confidence, as if it had been waiting for me to ask. I was delighted and intrigued.

I'd been toying with the idea of writing another book for a while but this time, I wasn't sure where to start. On a whim, I typed:

'I'd like to write a book on this topic. Can you help me structure it?'

The AI responded instantly:

'Of course! Would you like an outline, key messages, or draft chapters to get started?'

I was hooked.

I'd already written two books *the old-fashioned way*. Now it felt like I had found a way to sidestep the hardest parts of writing – effortless, efficient, almost too good to be true.

Within days, I had what looked like an entire book – structured chapters, compelling stories, clear key messages. It was efficient, seamless and oddly satisfying. I felt productive. Accomplished even.

But when I returned to it a few days later, something felt off.

The words were there, but the thinking wasn't. The ideas were neat but lifeless.

It wasn't just missing my voice – it was missing the struggle, the insight, the hard-won connections that make something real.

I tried to fix it.

I tweaked the chapters, added my own reflections, adjusted the language. But no matter how hard I tried, I couldn't find the thread – the invisible line that connects one idea to the next, the thread that comes from wrestling with a problem, turning it over, sitting with the discomfort of not knowing.

That thread wasn't there because *I* hadn't created it. *AI had.*

So, I started again.

This time, I was more deliberate. I gave it clearer instructions, defined the key messages and outlined the chapters myself. I thought I was in control. But slowly, almost without noticing, I found myself relying on the ease of asking complex questions and accepting simple answers.

Not once, but multiple times.

I wrote multiple books with AI. Each one looked polished, structured, convincing. But beneath the surface, they were hollow - generic shells of something real. The kind of writing that sounds impressive until you scratch just a little and then it crumbles.

I'd fallen into **The Answer Trap.**

Not because of AI itself, but because of something deeper - something instinctive. My enthusiasm for quick answers, my craving for clarity - the reassurance that I was on the right path - my desire to feel like I was making 'real' progress pulled me in.

And AI? It simply gave me what I wanted: Answers. Fast, confident, convincing answers.

But the real danger wasn't in the answers. It was in how easily (and unwittingly) I stopped thinking for myself.

It's not just me. We all fall into The Answer Trap every day, often without realising it.

- Have you ever been asked a question by a child, only to realise you didn't actually know the answer - but answered anyway?
- Have you ever been in a meeting where someone asked a complex question and instead of pausing to think, you said something that sounded right to avoid looking incompetent?
- Have you made an important decision and then, a while later, thought to yourself *'That was such a bad idea. What was I thinking?'*

- Have you pressed send on an AI-generated email without pausing to question whether the message was what you really wanted to say?

That's The Answer Trap. And it's everywhere.

ABOUT THIS BOOK

The Answer Trap is not about writing books and it's definitely not just about AI.

It's about our relationship with uncertainty and how we navigate it – at work, in life, in teams and in society.

It's about moving beyond default thinking so we can gain the clarity we need to make better choices and navigate chronic disruption with confidence.

This book is also about how, in a world that's becoming more complex, we're drawn to anything that feels simple. How our craving for clarity – combined with tools designed to give us instant answers – can quietly strip away the very thing that makes us human: the ability to wrestle with uncertainty, to question deeply and to think intentionally.

And, our ability to do so together.

Why it matters

We're standing at a crossroads.

The window to shape our relationship with AI and uncertainty is closing. Every time we choose *default* over *deliberate* thinking, we reinforce a habit that is silently and permanently shaping our future. Not just yours or mine – but that of humanity.

AI isn't the enemy. It's an extraordinary tool - fast, powerful and capable of synthesising information in ways we never imagined.

AI already raises many questions.

- What is it?
- How do we use it?
- How do we get the most out of it?

But there is a bigger, more important question and it isn't about AI's capabilities. The question is this.

- What happens when we let AI do the heavy cognitive lifting *for* us instead of *with* us?

But why is this so important?

In turbulent times, the more we default to quick, confident answers, the easier it becomes to stop thinking critically, curiously and creatively. Not because we're lazy or careless, but because it feels efficient and productive. It feels safe.

It makes us feel *in* control when the world feels increasingly *out* of it.

But over time, that convenience comes at a cost: the slow erosion of the very thing that makes us adaptable, innovative and capable of navigating complexity. And it is happening at the very time in human history when we need it more than ever.

I call it the *Dodo Effect*.

Dodos weren't dumb, they simply *de*volved a survival skill (ie. the ability to fly) because they had no natural predators and thus, no need to maintain it. Then, when humans brought their domesticated animals, the Dodos didn't stand a chance.

When it comes to AI, we still have a choice. We can use it to make our thinking better, or… we can let it do our thinking for us.

The time to choose is now.

What to expect

This isn't a book about optimising routine tasks. You're already good at that.

This is about the moments that pull you off track, throw you off balance or quietly shut down your best thinking.

But this book aims to do more than just help you navigate complexity and make better choices; it will change how you *reclaim control of your thinking* in a world that rewards speed over depth.

You'll learn practical strategies to help you recognise and break free from The Answer Trap and empower others to do the same.

But beyond that, this book is about rewiring the way you engage your brain when the pressure is high, and the path unclear.

We all have an extraordinary mind: the part that is drawn to an intriguing conundrum, gets excited by a mystery and finds deep satisfaction in uncovering something truly new. But in a world of fast, easy answers, that part of our thinking is quietly being switched off.

This book is here to turn it back on.

Your map out of the trap

One of the most important elements of this book is its practicality. After all, what's the point in sharing conceptual theories if there is no way to apply them to what is happening in your world?

Throughout the book you'll find 'Make it real' sections, designed to help you apply the ideas or concepts being discussed. Reading them provides a good start. However, if you really want to build your cognitive muscles, I recommend pressing 'pause' and actually doing the exercises as we go.

Another critical element of the book is 'the map'. This captures the essence of what you need to know and shows how the different parts of the book build on each other. More importantly, once you've finished the book 'Your Map Out of The Trap' will be the practical tool that helps you work out where you are and what to do next.

YOUR MAP OUT OF THE TRAP

1

CATCH THE TRAP

CHANGE YOUR PARADIGM

SEE THE SYSTEM

FEEL THE RIP

2

MAKE THE SWITCH

FLIP THE LID

SPOT YOUR DEFAULT

SHIFT TO COPILOT

3

MASTER *YOUR* MOMENT

NAVIGATE

ARTICULATE

ACTIVATE

4

IGNITE SHARED MOMENTUM

ALIGN

ACCELERATE

CULTIVATE

What you'll discover

As we go, you'll be introduced to The Moment Method: a practical approach to thinking clearly in pressure and complexity.

We'll also explore the five core thinking modes: Doing, Solving, Learning, Exploring and Sensemaking; and begin to understand how your brain moves between them when disruption strikes.

You'll discover the default pattern your own brain falls back on under pressure; it's the one that feels comfortable, productive and instinctive, but can quietly pull you off track.

And most importantly, you'll learn how to create the space, structure and strategies that allow you to stay in control of your thinking, even when the pressure rises.

Because when we learn to think differently as individuals, our clarity becomes the foundation for something bigger:

A new cognitive rhythm where human thinking and AI aren't in competition but in conversation, each enhancing the other.

Why?

Because when we stop competing with AI and start thinking alongside it, we unlock a new kind of intelligence: one where we evolve, rather than devolve.

And, when enough people stop settling for easy, obvious answers, we activate something far more powerful: the collective ability and energy to collaboratively navigate complexity with confidence, reclaim our own thinking and shape the future instead of just reacting to it.

So, that's where this journey begins. Let's get moving.

PART 1:

CATCH THE TRAP

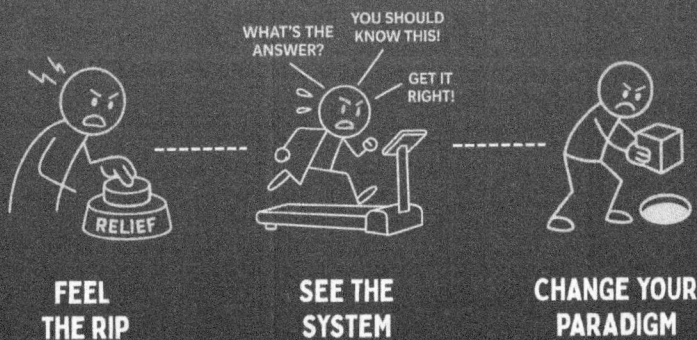

FEEL THE RIP

SEE THE SYSTEM

CHANGE YOUR PARADIGM

PART 1: WHAT TO EXPECT

Welcome to our starting point. Before we can talk about changing how we think, we first need to get honest about how we often operate, especially when the pressure is on. We need to truly see the subtle, powerful forces that pull even the smartest people off course.

This first part of our journey is all about awareness. It's about naming and understanding a phenomenon that affects us all: The Answer Trap. That instinctive and often unconscious leap towards relief and closure, particularly when faced with uncertainty, complexity or speed, rather than holding out for genuine clarity.

Over the next five chapters, we'll explore this trap from different angles. You'll build a crucial understanding of the trap from the inside out and uncover the compelling biological, psychological and environmental reasons as to why premature answers feel so right, even when they lead us astray.

We'll also trace the far-reaching consequences of staying stuck and discover the critical role that Artificial Intelligence plays as a modern-day accelerant of our addiction to answers.

Finally, we'll take a glimpse at the world beyond the trap and see the tangible difference and possibilities available when we can learn to break free.

Part 1 offers two essential ingredients. The ability to see The Answer Trap in different contexts, and a deeply compelling reason to break free.

So, let's dive into the deep end.

CHAPTER 1
THE RIP

Alex stares at her screen, fingers hovering over the keyboard. The email from the CEO is waiting. The messaging app notification is flashing. The supplier crisis is unfolding.

Her phone vibrates again, a frustrated text from her son complaining about his brother. Again.

Another issue, another fire to put out.

Her day? Already stacked with problems that weren't there yesterday. You know that feeling, right? Somewhere between overwhelm, frustration, and exhaustion.

That's where Alex is.

It's not just the sheer number of things; it's the weight of knowing that every decision, every answer, *matters*.

6:30am, her day started with a news alert: another market shock overnight.

By 8:00am, she'd put out three small fires and accidentally started a fourth. A key supplier in trouble, something about a cyberattack.

Her strategy, the one she spent months developing, is already at risk. A quiet churn in her gut. After months of planning, she can see it going off track before she even has time to respond. Outdated before it's even fully in motion.

Another vibration on her phone. Another demand.

With a deep sigh, Alex glances at her phone. Eight unread messages and a group chat from legal marked 'urgent'. A message from her partner: 'Can we talk later? I know you're busy.'

She swallows hard. She doesn't have time for any of it.

It's not just the pace; it's the unpredictability. The way everything is connected. Problems don't arrive one at a time, neatly packaged with clear solutions. Instead, they're ambiguous, they collide; pile up and morph into something bigger.

She *has* to act. Answers are needed, *now*. But beneath the surface urgency, a quieter question lingered: What was the *right* move?

INSIDE ALEX'S HEAD

Her brain's already moving faster than she can think.

What just happened? How bad is this? Who needs to know?

She clicks open the email from legal. Scans it but doesn't really read. Questions fire:

Could this be a contract issue? Are we exposed? How much risk are we carrying?

The CEO's email flashes again. Still unanswered.

What does she already know? What does she expect me to know? What's my next move?

She grips the edge of her desk, feels the pressure rising. She isn't paid to sit in indecision. She's paid to act. To *look* like she's making progress, even when it feels like pure pressure.

What should I do first?

The supplier crisis? Because without them, the business stalls. The CEO's email? Because Alex's credibility is on the line.

She can't afford to get this stuff wrong. Can't afford to wait. She just needs to pick a direction. *Any* direction.

A flicker of hesitation. Her finger hovers over the keyboard. She just wants this feeling to stop.

ALEX FALLS IN

She decides. She *has* to. Her fingers move.

Email to the supplier: 'We need an urgent risk assessment by lunchtime.'

Group message to her team: 'Looking into the supplier situation, more details soon.'

Forwarded report to the CEO: 'Attaching recent analysis, will update you shortly.'

Action taken. A wave of relief washed over her. For the first time that chaotic morning, she felt a flicker of control. The inbox a little clearer, the problems momentarily contained.

But had she actually *fixed* anything?

Or just reached for the first action that offered relief, just enough to feel in control and move on, regardless of whether it was truly the most useful response?

Alex doesn't have time to question it.

MAKE IT REAL

Have you ever been Alex? Not just at work – but in life? If you felt a flicker of discomfort reading her story, maybe even wanted it to end before it did… that's important. Don't rush past it - just pause.

Notice what that discomfort feels like in your body right now. Is it tension? Frustration? Urgency? What words would you use to describe it?

Write them down. This is the feeling that pulls us in.

_____

_____

_____

Key takeaway:

We don't fall into The Answer Trap when things are going smoothly. We fall in when they're not. Recognising that moment and how it feels, is your first signal. Learning to notice it is the first step in breaking free.

WHAT HAPPENED TO ALEX?

Let's zoom out on Alex's story. As we watch it unfold, we can see that the most useful thing for Alex to do would be to step back and take a breath. To look at the situation and attempt to understand what was really going on. She reacted instead, defaulting to *doing something*, not pausing to question the situation, or her actions.

So, why did Alex do that?

What she did was reasonable, given the pressure. But what she missed ran deeper. And, in the blink of an eye, she was already onto the next thing, caught in the current.

This is The Answer Trap.

When faced with a complex, ambiguous or high-pressure situation, it's the tendency to settle for the first plausible answer (regardless of whether it's right or wrong). Then, to stop thinking about it and move on.

It doesn't happen when we make a decision. It happens much earlier, in that subtle moment when we stop thinking – not because we've achieved genuine clarity, or progress, but simply because we've made the internal pressure stop.

We feel better, relieved, so we *assume* we've done the right thing, even if we haven't truly addressed the situation.

The Answer Trap doesn't feel like a mistake. Instead, it gives the impression of being decisive, like you're taking charge. But, what it truly rewards isn't clear thinking; it's simply a sense of 'being done'.

It's less about finding the right answer and more about grabbing the closest one that stops that uneasy feeling of not knowing. This makes us think we're moving forward, even if we're tackling the wrong issue, or just the obvious part.

Let's come back to Alex.

Did she fix the supplier crisis? Unlikely.

What she did was escape the immediate discomfort of feeling psychologically stuck: trapped in complexity, expected to act quickly, but without the space, structure or strategies her brain needed to think clearly first.

That's why The Answer Trap is so dangerous and insidious. The moment we land on an answer, *any* answer that provides relief, the internal pressure seems to disappear. *Phew!* Decompression.

The Answer Trap is relief masquerading as progress.

It tricks our brain. And, because we feel back in control, we often don't even notice we might be drifting off course. The danger isn't just overconfidence; it's that quiet moment when relief convinces us the thinking work is done. So, just when we might need our brain to stay engaged, to question deeper, it moves on, satisfied with the quick fix.

I know this feeling intimately.

As a corporate leader, as a parent and in my own consulting practice. I've made countless decisions that felt absolutely right in the heat of the moment, only to realise later, sometimes painfully, that I'd grabbed the easiest answer, not the best one. I'd prioritised relief over rigour.

This is the real risk.

> *We don't just make suboptimal choices; we get trapped in the illusion that we've made the right one, because the discomfort stopped. And then... we dig ourselves in and defend it.*

WHY WE DON'T SEE IT COMING: THE RIP CURRENT

Alex doesn't realise it yet, but she's being pulled by something deeper than a single decision. It's a thinking pattern, a cognitive undertow, that *feels* like forward motion but is quietly dragging her off course.

The Answer Trap is like a rip current at the beach.

It's often invisible on the surface. The water might look calm; everything seems under control. But underneath, unseen forces

– shifting assumptions, rising pressure, the brain's desire for certainty – are already at work.

Then, the pull starts.

An unexpected shift in the situation. A spike in pressure and the arrival of ambiguity. A moment where the right path forward isn't obvious, but the need to act feels overwhelming.

Your instinct, like a swimmer caught in a rip, is often to fight it directly: swim harder against the pull. Do something. *Anything* to get back to the perceived safety of solid ground.

You work harder. You push forward. You feel like you *must* be making progress, because you're exerting so much effort. And, the more energy you waste, the more exhausted you become.

But you're not gaining ground. You're actually being pulled further out, further away from where you intended to be.

The Answer Trap works in precisely the same way.

When our attempts to do something important are interrupted, creating ambiguity or complexity, we feel the pull – not necessarily panic, but intense pressure. A cognitive and emotional tension we're desperate to resolve.

So, we reach for the nearest answer, the quickest action, the most familiar solution, because like a swimmer grabbing for a flimsy piece of driftwood, it offers the illusion of safety and forward movement.

It *feels* like we're swimming back to shore.

But just like a real rip current, The Answer Trap doesn't usually drag us under completely in one go; it subtly pulls us in the wrong direction. We end up parallel to the *real* challenge, working hard, but not actually addressing the core issue and drifting further from the best outcome.

And now, that current is stronger and more pervasive than ever, because the systems around us, especially digital tools and AI, aren't just fast. They are increasingly designed to give us answers that feel right, coherent and complete, often before we've even fully articulated the right question.

When we're under pressure, that kind of instant, confident output feels like blessed clarity.

Often, it's just another powerful pull in the current, we're miles off course.

LET'S COME BACK TO YOU

This isn't just about Alex, or leaders navigating corporate crises. It's about being human in a world that's often moving faster than our reflective thinking can keep up.

Whether you're leading a business, designing complex systems, raising a family or just trying to make sense of your own life and what's coming next, you've felt this pull. You've been caught in The Rip.

And here's where things get a little uncomfortable.

> *What if some of the decisions you trust most, the certainty you sometimes feel, the actions you take automatically every day aren't actually pulling you forward, but subtly pulling you off course?*

Not just in high-stakes meetings or moments of visible leadership failure. But in the small, everyday ways you respond to the unexpected, the ambiguous and the uncomfortable. For example:

- The way you quickly settle an argument just to restore peace, rather than exploring the underlying issue.

- The way you search the internet for immediate reassurance when faced with doubt, instead of sitting with the uncertainty for a moment.

- The way you push forward with a familiar plan, not because you're convinced it's still right, but because stopping, questioning and potentially changing course feels more confronting than quietly following a flawed trajectory.

- The way you avoid asking a potentially disruptive question at work, because you don't want to be perceived as 'slowing things down', or 'not being a team player'.

- The way you choose the familiar framework, process, or routine, because building, or trying something new feels too effortful, too uncertain, too exposed… even if the old way isn't really working anymore.

Have you ever made a decision, big or small, and weeks, months, or even years later, had that moment of uncomfortable clarity: *'What on earth was I thinking?'*

Perhaps it was a significant choice at work.

Maybe you had to decide whether to scale back an ambitious initiative your team was passionate about. On the surface, it looked like a resourcing issue. But beneath it churned personal investment, stakeholder expectations, shifting priorities and maybe a hidden fear that admitting limitations would look like failure. So, you pushed ahead, keeping the project alive on paper, even though you suspected it was doomed.

Or maybe it was quieter.

You gave tacit agreement in a meeting to a decision you had reservations about. Not because you *believed* in it, but because asking a question, potentially triggering debate, or discomfort, felt too hard in that moment. Easier to just go along.

Perhaps you faced a major personal decision with complex trade-offs, like moving cities, or changing careers and you defaulted to the option that felt like forward momentum, even if it wasn't necessarily in the right direction for you deep down.

On paper, it might have made logical sense. But underneath, maybe you *knew* the timing was off, or the fit wasn't quite right. But you said yes anyway, because saying no, or saying 'I need more time to think,' felt too uncertain. Too messy. Too difficult to explain.

When you look back honestly, you probably *knew* something felt 'off' at the time. You might not have had the precise words for it, but some part of you sensed the misalignment, the compromise and the avoidance.

Still, you moved forward. Because stopping, questioning, sitting with the discomfort? That felt harder.

Let's peek beneath the surface of your specific moment like that.

MAKE IT REAL

Looking back on your example:

Was your decision primarily driven by a genuine search for the best possible path forward, or by that uncomfortable, urgent desire to simply make the uncertainty, or the pressure go away?

_____

_____

_____

Did you choose the answer, or action that fitted the situation *best*, or the one that simply offered the quickest sense of closure and allowed you to move on?

_____

_____

_____

And, if you'd felt able to pause then and truly *look* at the situation differently without the immediate pressure for relief, might you have chosen a different path?

_____

_____

_____

And the most important question… Why? Why did you choose the way you did? What was the underlying need that your brain was trying to protect, or satisfy in that moment?

_____

_____

_____

Key takeaway:

In complex and ambiguous situations, it can feel like we have no choice but to 'take a punt' because the information we need isn't there. And sometimes, that's true. But often, the insight we need is already available. However, because it's not immediately obvious we don't see it and, we don't stay there long enough to take a closer look.

So why *don't* we stop? Why don't we look?

Or, at least, why do we stop looking before we have what we truly need? You might tell yourself 'I didn't have enough time', or 'There were too many unknowns', or 'I had to be decisive'. And those things may *feel* true.

Underneath it all, was that a conscious assessment, or an automatic feeling that drove the action? Were you making the decision the situation needed, or the decision *you* needed emotionally, because doing so would bring the difficult moment to a comfortable, quick close?

In these critical moments, we don't stop thinking because we're not smart enough. We often stop thinking because our brain feels stuck, overwhelmed or threatened by the ambiguity and it desperately wants that feeling to end. So, it instinctively grabs the nearest, easiest, most plausible-seeming answer. One that doesn't necessarily fix the *real* problem. It just gives us the *feeling* that we've solved it.

That is **The Answer Trap**. It's not rare. It's not reserved for high-stakes corporate blunders. It happens to all of us, subtly and frequently. And it's always there, waiting for that moment of pressure, when something important feels like it's under threat.

In a world that's only getting faster, louder, more complex and more saturated with instant answers… escaping it is no longer just a helpful skill. It's a necessity.

HOW DO WE BREAK FREE?

If The Answer Trap is like a powerful, invisible rip current pulling us off course, how do we learn to recognise it earlier? How do we resist that instinctive urge to just swim harder against it, or grab the first piece of driftwood (the easy answer) that floats by? Especially in a world that constantly rewards speed and confident certainty?

In an era where AI can generate plausible answers in milliseconds, the real human advantage, the critical edge, isn't trying to find answers faster. It's developing the courage and the skill to pause, to challenge assumptions (including our own) and to ask the one insightful question that might change everything.

As you've probably gathered, this book isn't just about explaining The Answer Trap. It's designed to show you what it *feels* like to be caught in it and more importantly, what it feels like to begin resisting its pull. Not just once, but consistently, in those everyday moments where pressure and complexity conspire to hijack your best thinking. Especially in the moments that truly matter.

And now, having felt the reality of the trap, it's time to understand it's underlying mechanics, so it stops working so automatically on you.

That's what the next chapter is all about.

MAKE IT REAL

Today, just try to catch one moment when you feel that internal urge to act fast, find a quick solution or make an immediate judgment, perhaps when feeling slightly pressured or uncertain.

Don't change anything. Don't judge yourself. Just pause internally for a single breath and ask yourself: Am I reaching for this answer (or action) because it's genuinely the most thoughtful response, or primarily because it brings relief from this uncomfortable feeling?

Key takeaway:

The very first step in escaping The Answer Trap isn't doing something different. It's simply noticing the pull – before it drags you unknowingly into the current.

THIS CHAPTER IN A NUTSHELL

- The Answer Trap is a survival response, not a thinking failure. Under pressure, we reach for relief, not clarity.

- Relief feels like progress but often isn't. We mistake feeling better for being on the right track.

- The trap rewards closure over curiosity. Fast action feels like control but can pull us quietly off course.

- It shows up everywhere. From work to home, we often choose what's familiar or fast, not what's needed.

- Like a rip current, the trap is subtle but powerful. It doesn't drag us down; it pulls us in the wrong direction.

- The rise of AI is making the pull stronger. Faster answers increase the risk of premature certainty.

- Breaking free starts with staying with the question and resisting the urge to move on too soon.

CHAPTER 2

WHY THE ANSWER FEELS SO RIGHT, EVEN IF IT'S WRONG

When the Covid pandemic hit, I was working for myself and within a week, every single client engagement was cancelled. Every strategy session, keynote and leadership retreat? Stopped.

I was living in Melbourne, one of the most locked-down cities in the world.

Stuck inside. No work. Nowhere to go.

So, I did what many smart, capable people do under pressure: I leapt into action.

In just eight weeks, I designed and built CoronaCommunities, a platform intended to help neighbours coordinate support for each other during lockdown. It seemed comprehensive at the time, including a map-based onboarding system, online training for coordinators, community guidelines, safety protocols and email templates. I developed messaging channels, video briefings, digital infrastructure, principles of participation and tools for better on-line conversations.

It was thoughtful. Detailed. Values-driven. But there was one major problem.

I never asked the most important question: Is this what people actually want or need right now?

Instead, I assumed. I created. I pushed forward. Because doing something felt better than doing nothing. Movement felt like momentum and productivity felt like purpose.

Eventually, I reached out to a few local Facebook community group leaders to share the idea.

No response.

They were already managing things their way. I happened to run into my neighbour one day while putting out the bins. I explained CoronaCommunities with pride. He smiled kindly and said, 'Oh… we're already using a neighbourhood WhatsApp group – I'll send you the link.'

That was the moment it hit me.

I'd poured eight intense weeks into a solution that wasn't needed. I'd built something for a problem that had already been solved, just not in the way I thought it should be. And while I was busy doing,

I wasn't listening or looking. I wasn't asking and I wasn't adapting in real-time.

I was stuck in The Answer Trap, throwing effort at uncertainty in the hope that something would stick.

It didn't.

CoronaCommunities never went live. My business took another 18 months to recover. But the lesson stuck with me. Even smart, well-intentioned people fall into the trap, especially under pressure.

It's not about whether you're good at solving problems;
it's about whether you're using the right kind of
thinking for the moment you're in.

That's the difference between creating momentum and misfiring, progressing and burning out, or insight and regret. Sometimes, though, the trap starts much earlier.

WHY THE ANSWER FEELS SO RIGHT, EVEN IF IT'S WRONG   39

WHERE THE TRAP BEGINS

Ishika sat at the kitchen table, watching her son frown at his homework. His shoulders were hunched, his pencil tapping the page with frustration.

'Mum, this doesn't make sense,' he said.

'What doesn't?' she asked, leaning over.

'This question,' he pointed. "What is the main reason the Roman Empire collapsed?' But there isn't just one reason. There were, like, ten things that happened. The book says politics, economics, the military, disease... So, which one is the answer?'

Ishika scanned the multiple-choice options. Sure enough, one answer was required.

'Well,' she said gently, 'What do you think?'

He hesitated. 'I think it was a mix of everything. But that's not the answer they want, is it?'

That sentence hit her like a punch to the stomach. Not just as a mother, but as an experienced executive who had spent years working with leaders trained to do the same thing.

This was The Answer Trap in its earliest form.

Her son had already learned that school wasn't necessarily about thinking. It was often about guessing what answer the system wanted. He wasn't being rewarded for curiosity. He was being taught to suppress it.

> *The cost wasn't just getting a question wrong. The cost was learning, slowly and quietly, that complexity should be ignored if it doesn't fit the box.*

Ishika put her arm around him and smiled. 'You're right. There isn't just one answer. But sometimes, school isn't about thinking. It's about showing that you can play by the rules.'

He slumped. 'That's stupid.'

She laughed softly. 'It is. But here's the trick: Never stop thinking... even when the system wants you to.'

This wasn't just about kids. It was the same habit she'd seen in boardrooms, strategy retreats and executive teams: smart adults reaching for what 'sounded right' because they'd learned, long ago, that exploring complexity was risky.

The thing about The Answer Trap is that it doesn't *feel* like a trap. But underneath that satisfying rush, something deeper is happening.

Let's explore what's really going on here.

THE ILLUSION OF PROGRESS

Remember that moment Alex hit send in Chapter 1?

Her shoulders dropped. Her breathing slowed and for a second, the chaos felt manageable. That wasn't clarity. That was her brain giving her a hit of relief. Just like mine did, every time I ticked something off the CoronaCommunities list. It *felt* like momentum.

It wasn't.

When we land on an answer, *any* answer, the brain interprets it as safety. The Anterior Cingulate Cortex (ACC), a part of the brain that fires up when there's conflict or uncertainty, powers down. The cognitive burglar alarm shuts off and we feel calmer.

This is because our brains are wired to seek clarity for survival. When uncertainty spikes, especially in moments of crisis, the amygdala, our brain's threat detector, lights up. That rising tension you feel. It's the brain interpreting ambiguity as risk. This makes 'not knowing' feel unsafe.

So, what does the brain do?

It often grabs the first available answer, not necessarily because it's correct, but because landing on *something* helps us feel like we're back in control. The faster we lock onto an answer, the faster the brain *seems* to believe the danger has passed, even if it hasn't.

Daniel Kahneman's foundational research adds another layer.

In his book *Thinking, Fast and Slow*, he described two modes of thinking: System 1 (fast, automatic, efficient) and System 2 (slow, deliberate, effortful). Under pressure, we naturally default to System 1. We lean on what's familiar or immediately available.

That's not laziness; it's energy conservation. But, if we never pause to engage System 2, we might never question whether we're focusing on the *real* challenge or just escaping the discomfort of not knowing.

Every time we land on an answer, our brain *can* give us a little re- ward. The tension drops. Perhaps there's a small dopamine hit. And for a fleeting moment, we feel smart, capable and in control. That's seductive, especially when the stakes are high.

In fast-moving, disrupted environments, we're rarely given the time, space or strategies to do the deeper thinking that today's chronically complex situations demand. So instead, we often con- serve energy.

We project confidence and we convince ourselves that we've en- gaged in System 2 thinking. In reality, we've stuck with System 1, grabbed the answer that *looked* closest to right, then, run with it.

This is reinforced by what researchers like Dunning and Kruger found. They discovered that people who lack expertise in an area can often feel the *most* confident, not because they're right, but be- cause they don't know enough to recognise what they've missed. That illusion of certainty is part of the trap's allure.

The systems we live and work in, whether formal workplaces, volunteer groups or public services, often compound this.

Certainty is rewarded. Speed *looks* like competence. Doubt feels dangerous. From classrooms to boardrooms, we're often taught to value quick solutions over deep understanding. Over time, we can learn to equate doubt with weakness and internalise the trap: it often feels better to sound sure than to pause and think.

When you walk away from a decision with that tight feeling in your chest, the one that whispers, 'something's not quite right,' you've been here. You've felt the trap.

Between our biology (like the ACC's alarm system, the amygdala's fear response and our System 1 reflexes) and our social training (through schools, workplaces and leadership norms), we're practically programmed to grab an answer.

That's why The Answer Trap can be so hard to detect. It rarely feels like we're doing something foolish. It feels like we're doing exactly what we're supposed to.

The real challenge isn't that we occasionally reach the wrong answer; it's that we often stop looking for it the instant we feel relief. Breaking free demands more than just telling yourself to 'think differently.'

As Adam Grant suggests, 'Thinking again is not a failure. It's a mark of flexibility and wisdom.' It's about questioning everything we've absorbed: that quick solutions signal competence, that hesitation is weakness and that uncertainty means ignorance.

It's hard enough when one person falls into The Answer Trap. However, what happens when whole teams, systems or societies do?

That's where we go next.

MAKE IT REAL

Today, notice a moment where someone offers a quick answer and everyone moves on. It might be in a meeting, a group chat or even just making dinner plans.

Watch what happens next. Does the group relax? Does the question disappear? Does it feel like progress?

_____

_____

_____

Now ask yourself: Was that answer right, or just fast, familiar or satisfying enough to bring relief?

_____

_____

_____

Key takeaway:

The more you consciously look for The Answer Trap happening around you, the more easily you'll be able to see it. And the more you notice it 'out there', the better you'll become at catching it in yourself.

CHAPTER IN A NUTSHELL

- The Answer Trap rewards relief, not clarity. We grab answers to ease discomfort, not necessarily to solve the real problem.

- It's not primarily a thinking failure. It's often a survival response, triggered by uncertainty and reinforced by how our brain and culture work.

- Fast answers feel good. Our brain releases tension, organisations reward speed and confidence gets mistaken for competence.

- Systems train us to reach for closure. From classrooms to boardrooms, we're often taught to value quick solutions over deep understanding.

- The trap becomes invisible. Because it feels like momentum, we rarely question if we're moving in the right direction.

- Seeing the trap is the first step. It gives us the space to choose a different kind of thinking: one that's slower, deeper and ultimately more useful.

CHAPTER 3
THE REAL COST

By now, you've seen how The Answer Trap works. You've felt the pull of fast relief, the speed of certainty and the strange comfort of something that feels right but isn't. But what does it actually cost us, day to day, moment to moment?

That feeling of relief is powerful and in a world that keeps us constantly on the hop it is little wonder we grasp for it. But was it the right decision? Or just the nearest exit?

We're not running from the work.

We're running from the weight of not knowing – the internal pressure of uncertainty, the mental exhaustion of navigating a world that demands answers faster than our brain can actually make sense of the situation.

Over time, this pressure takes its toll. It's more than just decision fatigue; it's a creeping cognitive shutdown, a learnt sense of overwhelm where our brains, seeking relief, start to favour shortcuts.

THE REAL COST 47

Under pressure, our thinking narrows. We don't just think faster; we think smaller. So, even when the situation needs broader thinking, we're already halfway to the nearest answer.

THE REAL PROBLEM

Sometimes, the way we *see* a problem is the real problem. To see how this plays out in everyday situations, consider this simple story from a primary school classroom.

It was just before lunch at the local primary school and it was reading time. The teacher gave the instructions: 'Go and grab your reading books and find a partner. Then, sit down quietly and take turns reading to each other.'

Five minutes later, most of the children were paired up, books open, voices murmuring through the pages. But one boy stood alone in the middle of the room, yelling at the top of his voice. The teacher marched over, irritation flickering across her face. 'Why are you yelling?' she asked, her voice firm.

The boy, unfazed, explained: 'I couldn't find a reading partner. I looked for one, but everyone was taken. I was yelling 'I don't have a partner!' so that anyone else who needed one would know.'

The teacher frowned. 'Do you think standing in the middle of the room and shouting is the best way to find a partner?'

The boy paused. 'Not really,' he admitted. 'But what would be better?'

'Well,' said the teacher, 'You could go up to people and ask them quietly.'

The boy's face twisted in confusion. 'But that wouldn't be more effective at all,' he argued. 'I'd have to interrupt people who already had partners. That wastes time for me and for them.'

The teacher opened her mouth, then hesitated. She could see his point. After a moment, she said, 'Alright. This lunchtime, I want you to think of a better way to do this, one that doesn't involve yelling.'

The boy nodded and ran off to lunch. When the bell rang, he returned, eyes shining with triumph. 'I've got the perfect way!' he announced. 'When it's time to find a partner, anyone who doesn't have one should go stand in that corner. That way, everyone will know, and the right people can find each other.'

It was simple, obvious, at least once someone had thought about it. From that day forward, the entire school adopted it.

The Answer Trap in action

The teacher's reflex was to correct the boy's approach based on social norms. The boy's instinct was to default to what felt like the most direct solution: being louder. Both were caught in their own version of The Answer Trap, settling on the first solution that made sense from their perspective, without stopping to properly define the real need or consider if there was a better way. The problem wasn't a lack of intelligence or effort. It was that they didn't question how they'd first framed the issue before moving forward.

And that's exactly what keeps us trapped.

THE PERSONAL COSTS

The impact of The Answer Trap might not be immediately obvious. You'll often feel it internally and start to question your own judgement. Alternatively, you may not notice it at all and remain totally convinced that the answer you have is the one (and only one) you need.

Leaders, in particular, find the trap harder to spot, because the pressure to appear confident often overrides the permission to think clearly.

You might find yourself second-guessing even small choices.

For example, whether to speak up in a meeting or push back on a decision that doesn't sit right. Or, you may start avoiding conversations that might get messy or slow things down, saying 'It's fine' when you suspect it isn't, just to keep things moving.

This can erode your confidence in your own thinking, even after you've made a call. You replay decisions later, wondering if you missed something obvious or worrying if you're just not sharp enough anymore.

The trap can make us shy away from complexity, reaching for the quick fix over wrestling with the open question, favouring what sounds good or seems practical rather than digging for what feels true.

We default to what's worked before – saying yes when we really mean maybe or writing the proposal we think they want to see. We stick with the familiar template, framework or process, because stepping into the unknown feels too effortful and too uncertain. And when things inevitably don't go to plan, we might blame ourselves. We wonder why we can't keep up. Why we feel stuck. Why everything feels harder than it used to.

This erosion of clear thinking might feel like a personal struggle, but the insidious thing about The Answer Trap is that it doesn't stay personal. It spreads through teams, professions, institutions and society, fragmenting shared understanding, flattening constructive challenge and replacing depth with superficial alignment. Its costs become harder to see and even harder to reverse.

THE COLLECTIVE COSTS

When The Answer Trap takes hold in a group, the damage isn't always obvious. People still talk, meetings still happen and progress still *seems* to be made. But underneath, alignment falters. Individual thinking, even when well-intentioned, fails to connect. It's a phenomenon I call 'cognitive fragmentation' that we'll explore in more detail later.

Everyone responds to the pressure in their own way. Some push forward to maintain momentum at all costs. Others hold back, quietly unsure but unwilling to voice doubt, while still others fix small, tangential things, avoiding the real, messy issue altogether.

So, on the surface, the group looks aligned, maybe even efficient, but each person is unconsciously dealing with a slightly different problem.

This leads to friction – not always loud disagreement, but quiet disconnection, missed moments of understanding, decisions interpreted differently and work that subtly goes off track. The lack of a shared focus – what we'll later emphasize as a 'shared moment' – means the team moves faster, but not together.

People shape their input around what feels safe, contributing just enough to keep things moving, but not enough to risk slowing things down with challenging questions.

It's not that they've stopped thinking. It's that they've stopped thinking *together*. Soon, they're not tackling the real issue anymore. They're managing perceptions, keeping things moving and trying to maintain a sense of progress.

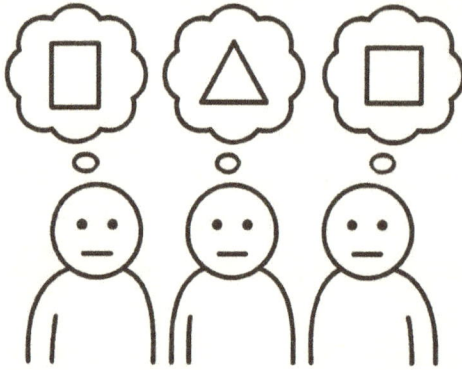

That progress is fragile, because the deeper, shared understanding needed to anchor it never happened. This is how smart teams get stuck. Not because they aren't capable, but because the pressure to decide quickly, move cleanly and appear aligned becomes stronger than the pull toward deeper, collaborative thinking.

The Answer Trap doesn't just flatten thinking, removing nuance. It fragments it. To escape this, as we'll later see, we need to deliberately cultivate 'shared moments' of thinking together.

THE CULTURAL COSTS

These fragmented patterns, repeated over time, begin to shape the culture of any group, team or organisation – ultimately impacting the experience of the individuals within it.

People stop raising objections, not necessarily because they've changed their minds, but because they feel it's unproductive or even risky.

Differences in perspective get smoothed over and challenging the status quo gets labelled as being difficult. The longer this goes on, the more it becomes the accepted way of operating.

As a result, individuals may feel that their voice isn't heard, that the same few people dominate discussions. They see decisions made quickly, only to be quietly revisited or reworked later in smaller, informal settings, leaving them feeling excluded from key conversations. Meetings become an exercise in ticking off agenda items, but genuine connection and meaning dwindle.

The Answer Trap doesn't just derail a single conversation; it reshapes the culture of how people work together.

This means that even well-intentioned efforts can fall apart, leaving individuals confused and frustrated. Everyone believes they're focusing on the same thing and aligned with their colleagues, when in reality they're not. By the time this misalignment becomes clear, the opportunity for genuine clarity has often passed.

This is the longer-term human cost of The Answer Trap in groups. It goes beyond one-off disruptions or situations. Not only do groups regularly miss the best answer; individuals feel unheard and disempowered.

> *Before long, you're left with a collection of smart, exhausted people doing their best, but pulling in fundamentally different directions.*

This is how good work unravels: not from malice, but from a lack of shared understanding.

The pressure to move quickly and project certainty gradually re-shapes how people relate to one another. Over time, it erodes trust among individuals, stifles their willingness to express dissenting views and makes it increasingly difficult to have the kind of open, collaborative conversations that ambiguous, dynamic challenges demand.

HOW IT HAPPENS IN REALITY

A few years ago, I worked with a well-respected global organisa-tion grappling with a high-stakes regulatory shift. The change de-manded a fundamental rethink of how the business operated across borders, silos and legacy structures. It felt overwhelming from the start.

This was the first time the organisation had attempted such a sweeping transformation driven from the corporate centre. Expertise existed in pockets scattered across the globe, but there was no *shared understanding*, no *common language for thinking together* about how to navigate this level of change across the entire system.

Pressure mounted quickly and cracks began to appear.

A massive program was launched. Deadlines loomed and exter-nal consultants were brought in. Urgency quickly overtook clarity, and a flurry of activity outpaced the desire for coherent direc-tion. People felt adrift; the program didn't feel owned by those who had to implement it. The top-down approach clashed with a decentralised 'don't tell us what to do' culture. Key stakeholders felt confused or disengaged, retreating into their silos.

Everyone was incredibly busy, churning out reports and attending meetings, but the core purpose felt hollow. What made it worse was the quiet cognitive fragmentation.

> *Ask ten people what the program was really for, and you'd get ten different answers.*

Some saw it purely as a compliance exercise. Others believed it was a chance to transform risk management. This lack of *shared understanding* led to each leader and team member acting based on their own interpretation.

So, everyone delivered something, believing they were helping. But underneath, they were pulling in different directions, sometimes unknowingly duplicating effort or creating conflicting processes. Progress looked real on dashboards and status reports, but the foundations were fracturing.

After two years, tens of millions of dollars and many burnt reputations, the program was quietly closed. The most basic compliance work had been done, just enough to satisfy the minimum requirements. The sense of crisis had passed.

But what was left behind wasn't enhanced capability or transformation. It was confusion. A tangled legacy of mismatched processes, frustrated stakeholders and a deeper, lingering mistrust of enterprise led change initiatives.

The trap was set before any money was spent, but no one saw it happen. So when the program closed, no one really knew what went wrong.

There were plenty of theories, some expressed with considerable volume and confidence. Most put it down to poor decisions, yet in reality, it was the thinking behind them, that was the real culprit.

THE SYSTEMIC AND SOCIETAL COSTS

The impact of The Answer Trap extends far beyond individual interactions and group dynamics. When its patterns become embedded in the operating systems of entire professions, institutions and societies, the consequences are even more profound.

In fact, when societies gravitate toward simple answers for complex problems, they do more than sidestep complexity; they reshape how people think, relate and decide together.

It trains us to default to what's efficient, presentable and defensible, rather than what's thoughtful, honest and truly useful. And it's not just behaviour. It becomes embedded in how people work, how they're perceived and even what they believe about themselves and their capabilities. It shapes credibility and deeply impacts professional identity.

Research suggests that in environments where predictability and speed are highly valued, our brain's tolerance for ambiguity can actually decrease. We're not just thinking faster; we're potentially shrinking the cognitive and social space where good thinking, questioning and exploration can happen.

When entire professions and systems succumb to The Answer Trap, the results can be devastating. We see it in healthcare, where rigid adherence to guidelines can sometimes overshadow the nuanced needs of an individual patient. In education, where a focus on standardised testing can overshadow genuine learning; and in public policy, where appearances can outweigh long-term impact.

By the time someone summons the courage to say, 'Maybe we're asking the wrong question,' the plans are already locked in. People are invested, timelines are rolling and reputations are staked. The work isn't just moving; it's hurtling forward, even if no one is quite sure anymore if it's heading in the right direction.

You don't have to look far to see examples. Let's start with Brexit.

The UK's complex decision about its relationship with the European Union was reduced to a binary choice: leave or remain. The slogan 'Take back control' resonated powerfully, offering a simple, emotionally appealing answer in a moment of uncertainty. But beneath that surface clarity was a tangle of economic, political and social implications that are still playing out.

In the United States, Donald Trump's rise to power echoed a similar pattern. Complex global and domestic challenges involving immigration, trade and inequality were reframed as simple problems amenable to bold, confident solutions.

Whether the answers were practical or evidence based often seemed secondary to the fact that they sounded sure, decisive and easy to grasp.

When answers become part of a choreographed performance designed to project certainty, public discourse begins to fracture. Not necessarily because people stop caring, but because complexity stops getting sufficient airtime.

The underlying problems don't go away. They just get papered over with slogans, leaving the real thinking undone.

It's not just a modern problem.

History is full of examples where oversimplified thinking led to unintentional harm. In 1958, Mao Zedong launched the Four Pests Campaign in China, targeting sparrows as a key enemy of agricultural progress. The belief was simple: sparrows ate grain, so fewer sparrows meant more food. The campaign mobilised millions to eradicate the birds.

But sparrows didn't just eat grain; they also ate insects, particularly locusts. Without their natural predators, locust populations exploded. Crops failed and famine followed, leading to the deaths of millions. A campaign intended to solve hunger tragically made it far worse, not because people didn't care, but because they accepted a simplistic framing of the problem.

In a complex, interconnected system, that's not clarity. That's a trap.

I could give dozens more examples – different countries, different contexts – the above are far from unique. My point is that The Answer Trap scales rapidly and effectively. It's that bold, clear solution that bypasses complexity and unleashes consequences no one was prepared for.

The longer these patterns hold, the more they start to splinter the social fabric. People stop communicating effectively across differences because it feels too hard or pointless. Nuance gets mistaken for weakness or indecision. Debate degrades into division. Not necessarily because people want to fight, but because the shared understanding needed to have a constructive conversation has quietly disappeared.

We stop questioning what we think we know. We stop listening for what we might have missed. And in that silence, certainty becomes its own kind of echo chamber.

It's not a shared conclusion reached through thoughtful deliberation, but often a shared exhaustion. Everyone's shouting answers without a shared view of the question.

That's the cost to society.

Not just bad decisions, but a potential loss of our collective ability to think intentionally, to imagine creatively, to appreciate diversity and to act together with depth and foresight. We don't just lose perspective, we close off possibility.

MAKE IT REAL

Next time you're in a conversation where people are offering strong opinions or solutions, listen closely. Especially when you hear phrases like: 'We should definitely...' or 'The real issue is clearly...' or 'What we really need to do is...' Each one is an answer. But to what question? Ask yourself silently:

What question is this person really answering?

_____

_____

Is everyone in the conversation implicitly answering the same underlying question, or are they unknowingly answering a different one?

_____

_____

You won't always hear overt disagreement, but you might start to sense a deeper misalignment, a subtle feeling that people sound aligned on the surface but are thinking past each other underneath.

Later in the book, we'll explore specific techniques for catching this in the moment and how to make the real question visible before the competing answers take over. For now, just start noticing the pattern.

Key takeaway:

Every answer begins with a question. But too often, that question is assumed, unconscious or never spoken aloud. If we want to break free of The Answer Trap, we need to stop obsessing over the answer - and start paying attention to the question that comes before it.

THE AI FACTOR

These societal consequences are significant and now a new force is emerging that threatens to amplify The Answer Trap in unprecedented ways: Artificial Intelligence (AI).

The Answer Trap isn't new; we've always been drawn to the fastest way out of tension, especially in moments of pressure, uncertainty and complexity. The more disrupted the world becomes, the more our brains crave that relief.

AI doesn't just offer speed; it also offers the *appearance* of confidence, coherence and authority, even when its output is subtly biased, incomplete or simply incorrect. This combination of speed and authority creates a powerful pull towards premature closure.

And if we're not paying close attention, if we simply accept AI's output without critical engagement, it risks not only automating tasks but also subtly automating our thinking. It can provide plausible-sounding answers before we've even taken the time to formulate the right question – the one that gets to the heart of the matter.

That isn't mere acceleration; it's amplification. AI threatens to supercharge The Answer Trap, making the pull towards premature closure almost irresistible.

To navigate this new reality, we must get better, not just at using AI tools, but at cultivating flexible and fit-for-purpose thinking in a world where superficially convincing answers are always instantly available.

The Answer Trap is no longer a potential future problem; it's the current environment in which we're operating, often unconsciously.

Let's continue the conversation in the next chapter where we'll explore in detail the implications of AI for The Answer Trap and how we can safeguard our thinking in this new age.

CHAPTER IN A NUTSHELL

- The Answer Trap doesn't stay personal. It spreads through teams, professions, institutions and society.

- It fragments shared understanding, flattens constructive challenge and replaces depth with performative alignment.

- People don't stop thinking; they stop thinking together, often without realising it until it's too late.

- The trap rewards the appearance of momentum, even when the real question was never clearly defined or agreed upon.

- It scales insidiously. Each person thinks they're doing the right thing, but they're often answering different underlying questions.

- That's how systems drift into dysfunction: not with drama, but with quiet misalignment that compounds into confusion, exhaustion and rework.

CHAPTER 4
THE AI CHALLENGE

Human adoption of technology has been speeding up for decades, but the shift we're seeing today is on another level. The personal computer took 16 years to reach 100 million users. The internet took 7. The iPhone, about two and a half.

ChatGPT? Just 2 months. It didn't just land. It exploded.

And in that surge, something changed. Consumable AI didn't just enter the room. It started to shape how we think, emerging as a powerful accelerant of The Answer Trap.

When I say AI, I'm not talking about robots or sentient machines. I mean the tools that many of us now use daily - language models, content generators, chat interfaces, dashboards and predictive engines.

For me, using AI is like having a slightly over-eager colleague who never disagrees with you.

It offers structure before you're ready, fluency before you've earned it and clarity without the cognitive grind.

It's both thrilling and confronting. These accessible tools have shown me just how quickly I can fool myself into believing I'm thinking when I'm really just coasting.

Some days I love it. Other days, I want to strangle it. However, there's one critical and frankly, uncomfortable lesson. Using AI has taught me how easily I can confuse 'perceived' momentum with meaningful progress.

ANSWERS ON DEMAND

This is the seductive thing about AI, isn't it?

It delivers relief, a sense of forward motion and a perfect output. It does it quickly, often by mirroring your own style and preferences so convincingly that you don't notice you've stopped thinking.

My work is all about finding clarity to enable progress, especially when it's hard to come by. In particular, I focus on helping people to shift their mind into the right kind of thinking for the moment they're in.

I talked earlier about Daniel Kahneman and his foundational insights on System 1 and System 2 thinking. My work takes this to the next level, focusing on how our mind moves between the two systems, especially in times of complex disruption. I'm fascinated by:

• how we transition from fast to slow

- how we resist the pull of the obvious

- how to make System 2 more energising and less exhausting

It's all about enabling the brain to keep up with a world that never slows down and building the cognitive muscles to create clarity when nothing seems to be clear.

Yet, despite decades spent decoding cognitive 'stuckness' (and yes... I know it's not a real word) - I still fall into the trap. Especially when I'm using AI.

Why?

AI doesn't lead us astray with obviously bad answers.
It leads us astray with answers that sound brilliant.

Plausible, polished and close enough to the truth.

That's the danger. It's not about intelligence or discipline. It's about how our brains cope, especially when we're tired, pressured, confused or just desperate to feel like we're making progress.

AI doesn't just offer speed. It offers perceived clarity on tap. It bypasses curiosity, skips the pause and silences that essential wrestle with complexity. And that doesn't just change the answer. It changes what we think thinking actually is.

Despite their appearance, AI tools don't think, reason or understand. They predict. They rearrange patterns from vast amounts of data into something that looks like a good answer.

That's it.

To a tired or confused brain, a stretched team or a leader under pressure, that response doesn't look like a prediction. It looks like clarity. It sounds like insight and feels like confidence.

That's why it matters.

Often, we don't engage with these tools for what they are. We engage with them for what we need them to be in that moment.

A source of relief, a shortcut to progress or an end point. Something that sounds right so we can stop thinking and move on.

AI delivers that, not maliciously and not always inaccurately – but quickly, fluently and friction free.

WHY IT FEELS SO RIGHT

Let's face it. There's something incredibly satisfying about getting a complete answer without having to wrestle for it. It just flows and feels finished. And in a world full of noise and friction, that feeling on its own can make us sigh in relief and move on.

However, as good as it is, that feeling isn't always a sign of truth or depth. Often, it's just a sign of relief – that same old relief that lures us into The Answer Trap.

AI is brilliant at giving us that feeling, right on cue. It mimics confidence. It offers structure, logic, even tone. It does so without the hesitation or doubt that comes with deeper thinking.

> *And when AI doesn't actually know? It doesn't pause. It simply pulls something plausible from its predictive patterns, wraps it in smooth language and presents it as a fact.*

That's a big deal. As humans we tend to equate smoothness with certainty and associate coherence with clarity. And sometimes, if we're honest, we trust what comes easily more than what demands something of us.

THE QUIET SURRENDER TO DRIFT

This is the risk. It's not just that AI changes how we write, present or work. It changes how we think - quietly, slowly, yet significantly.

The more we use tools that bypass effort, the less we tolerate the discomfort that comes with thinking. And that System 2 thinking, the kind that's needed when we land in the unknown, is often uncomfortable.

It's uncertain. It takes time. It requires wrestling with ideas, sitting with not knowing and staying curious even when you're under pressure to be sure.

But AI gives us a way to skip all of that. It hands us something finished and neat. Something that sounds perfectly fine.

Slowly, without even noticing, we start to drift.

In individuals, that drift shows up as a subtle impatience - the shrinking space between the question and the click. The creeping sense that we *should* already have the answer.

That discomfort is a signal many of us now override by habit.

In teams, the drift shows up as a slide into polish over clarity. Answers that sound impressive but are built on shaky foundations. Teams who move quickly but stop challenging each other's logic - because what they've produced already sounds good enough.

In organisations, the drift is deeper.

Performance reviews become AI-generated summaries. Risk analyses are turned into dashboards that hide the underlying complexity. Strategic thinking is replaced with succinct syntheses - helpful, maybe, but hollow if no one's still doing the hard work underneath.

And at a societal level? The drift becomes dangerous.

It leads to decisions which shape people's lives being made at pace - based on language that *looks* like insight, without any of the nuance or context that good thinking requires.

The drift is invisible because it resembles progress. But we're skipping the essentials of thinking: reflection, connection, context, tension, slow ideas, unfinished thoughts and doubt.

In the rip current of The Answer Trap, AI makes this pull feel good, deceptively suggesting you're getting somewhere.

And this isn't just theory.

Decades ago, researchers noticed something unexpected: IQ scores around the world were rising. Each generation was scoring higher than the last, particularly in areas linked to abstract thinking and complex reasoning. It became known as the Flynn Effect and for a while, it gave us hope that we were becoming better thinkers over time.

But then something changed.

In recent years, that upward trend has reversed. In several countries, the gains have not just slowed - they've started to decline. Researchers are still unpacking why, but many believe it's linked to how much we now outsource thinking. Less effort. More shortcuts. Fewer demands on our capacity to wrestle with complexity.

That's the risk we face now - not just a loss of knowledge, but a loss of the ability to think deeply. A slow erosion of cognitive resilience and our ability to stay in System 2 thinking for as long as is required.

This kind of erosion is almost impossible to notice, until it's already happened. You see? If we stop asking real questions, stop noticing what's missing and stop building the muscle of deliberate thought – we don't just drift.

We shrink.

WHAT IF WE DO NOTHING?

In the introduction, I said we're at a crossroads. This is it.

We could keep going on the path we're on – the easy answer of smooth, fast, low friction (a classic Answer Trap move). We could tell ourselves it's not that bad, that AI will never really replace human thinking and that we'll catch ourselves when it matters.

But let's not skip ahead. Instead, let's sit with the uncomfortable questions:

- *If we keep going like this, where does that path really take us?*
- *Where does it take you and those who come after you?*

The greatest risk is not that AI will become more powerful – but that we'll become more passive. We'll stop noticing when our thinking has been outsourced. And, worse, we'll stop caring whether we've done the thinking at all.

*In truth, if we keep going the way we are, the biggest
risk isn't that AI gets better at pretending to think. It's
that we stop bothering to do it ourselves.*

We're already seeing the signs. Reports that sound strategic but
are built from fragments. Workshops that feel productive but are
scripted by tools trained on yesterday's thinking. Entire meetings
where people defer to dashboards and prompts, rather than engaging with each other.

It all *looks* like thinking - but the hard bit is missing. And that's the
danger. Not just for leaders and not just for teams. For all of us.

Why?

Because if we lose the capacity - or the will - to hold space for
real thought when things get complex or ambiguous, we don't just
lose insight. We lose the ability to find a new path when the old
one is gone.

We also lose our ability to challenge assumptions, weigh consequences, and ask the questions that still need asking when the
answer looks too easy. We see questions like *Why? What if?* and
What are we missing? as being no longer necessary.

When that happens, we devolve.

THE DODO EFFECT

The real threat of AI isn't that it's becoming smarter. It's that we
might stop needing to be.

When a species evolves in an environment without predators, something strange happens. It begins to lose the traits it no longer uses. Muscles weaken. Senses dull. Reflexes slow. That's what happened to the dodo. It didn't die out because it couldn't adapt – it died out because it no longer needed to.

That's the risk we face now.

As AI takes on more of the cognitive heavy lifting, we may not notice the slow decline of the very capabilities that enabled human beings to rise above the rest. Not just deep, but flexible, thinking.

Our brain wants maximum reward for minimal effort. If a tool gives us the reward faster, without needing to put the work in, our brain begins to skip the effort altogether. We don't just outsource tasks. We outsource the muscle it takes to do them.

And slowly, we stop noticing what we've lost. That's the Dodo Effect. Not extinction by catastrophe, but by comfort. Not because we weren't smart, but because we stopped needing to be. And in the age of AI, that's the extinction risk we now need to be watching for.

IT'S NOT TOO LATE

This isn't a warning that ends in despair - it's a reminder that thinking is still ours to reclaim. But the window of opportunity is narrowing.

We don't have to reject AI. However, we do need to re-engage ourselves - consciously, deliberately - in the moments that matter. Not just to avoid the drift, but to reclaim the edge that AI can't replace: the part of us that wrestles with a problem, connects the dots and creates original, human meaning.

Join me in the next chapter, where we'll explore exactly what that looks like - and how to build it back.

MAKE IT REAL:

Next time you use AI to help you write, plan or decide something, pause before you move on. Ask yourself a few questions.

Did this work pass through the part of me that wrestles for meaning?

_____

_____

_____

Does the output just sound smart, or does it say something real and contextualised?

_____

_____

_____

If someone else had given me this exact output, would I trust it without further probing?

_____

_____

_____

Key takeaway:

You don't need to stop using AI - far from it. In fact, those who avoid it risk being left behind. However, using it well means engaging not just with the output, but with the thinking that shaped it. If you can't look away from the result and clearly explain the intention and context behind it, then it's worth pausing. Dig a little deeper because the real insight or opportunity may still be waiting.

CHAPTER IN A NUTSHELL

- AI doesn't just accelerate answers; it accelerates the feeling of being done.

- That's what makes it dangerous: not because it's wrong, but because it feels right enough to let us move on prematurely.

- It offers polish, pace and fluency that sound like progress, but can bypass the friction that real thinking requires.

- The risk isn't just poor decisions; it's a cultural drift from clarity to coherence, from sensemaking to formatting.

- We don't just stop thinking; we stop noticing that we've stopped.

- That's how a new, shallower standard for thinking gets set, not by force, but by fatigue and convenience.

- But we still have a choice, a chance to reset what good thinking looks like in the age of AI.

- That window is still open, but it won't stay that way forever. If we want to keep our edge, we must reclaim the thinking, on purpose.

CHAPTER 5
BEYOND THE ANSWERS

Everyone thought they knew the answer: stomach ulcers? Caused by stress, or maybe spicy food. At the time, it made intuitive sense.

People with ulcers often were stressed. They did change their diets. Antacids helped. The medical community reinforced this belief, reiterating it in textbooks, treatments and language, claiming ulcers were the body's way of saying 'slow down.'

Except they weren't.

In the early 1980s, Dr Barry Marshall, a gastroenterologist from Perth, refused to accept this 'obvious' answer. He and pathologist Dr Robin Warren discovered a spiral-shaped bacterium, *Helicobacter pylori*, in the stomachs of ulcer patients, seeing patterns no one else had paused long enough to see.

But no one wanted to hear it, because the existing answer didn't just feel right; it felt certain, comfortable, familiar and deeply embedded.

So, Marshall did the unthinkable.

He drank a vial of the bacteria himself. Within days, he developed gastritis. Within weeks, the entire medical world had to rethink everything it thought it knew. Ulcers weren't stress induced. They were bacterial. Treatable. Curable.

The problem hadn't been a lack of knowledge. It was The Answer Trap itself: a whole system had built itself around the wrong answer and stopped questioning it.

This chapter isn't about ulcers. It's about what becomes possible when we stop grabbing the answer that *feels* safe and stay with the question that *is* real. It's about navigating our way out of *The Answer Trap* – something I've spent the last thirty years helping people, teams and organisations do and watching the amazing things that happen when they succeed.

I'm pleased to say that it doesn't require ingesting a vial of bacteria, or anything else for that matter! But it *does* require a willingness to sit a little longer than is comfortable with 'not knowing' an answer, and the preparedness to search for genuine clarity instead of leaping towards premature closure.

We've talked a lot about what it's like inside *The Answer Trap*. But, what's it like when you're able to break free?

THE SHIFT WITHIN: A NEW KIND OF CLARITY

We tend to think of clarity as something that arrives in a flash – a sharp insight, a gut feel or a breakthrough moment. When you've been caught in The Answer Trap and your mind has been spinning, firefighting or just chasing the next quick win, clarity doesn't feel like a bolt of lightning.

It feels like a slow exhale, like silence after noise. It's the space where the urgency to do something subsides, replaced by a clearer perception of what truly matters.

You start noticing things you didn't see before (not because they weren't there, but because your brain was too busy reacting to register them). It's also where you ask different questions and pause conversations you would have rushed through. Why?

Because often the task you've been pushing up the list, the one that *feels* urgent, isn't actually the task that matters most.

> *When people break free of The Answer Trap at a personal level, what they describe isn't a master plan. It's space.*

They find the space to think clearly, to feel uncomfortable without reacting too quickly and to be clear without needing to pretend they are certain. From this space, you stop wasting energy trying to control the uncontrollable, fill every silence, or prove you're across everything all the time. You get better at seeing what's actually going on beneath the pressure, the noise and the urgency.

This shift enables your brain to change how it thinks, which changes how you decide and how you show up in the world. When you stop pressuring yourself (and others) for instant answers and start engaging with what truly matters, people notice.

They trust you more, not because you *have* all the answers, but because you demonstrate the ability to stay with the real questions. You move from reactive to strategic, from merely convincing to truly credible. That kind of influence comes from being able to release your grip on 'the need to know'.

★★★

So, as an individual, escaping The Answer Trap is powerful, but subtle. You don't suddenly become a genius. You become clearer, calmer and wiser.

Yet, as we've discussed, a new challenge, and opportunity, emerges. Once you've reclaimed your clarity, what do you do with it? How do you extend it? And, what happens when a tool like AI enters the scene?

THINKING WITH AI

AI isn't just another shiny distraction. Although currently in its infancy, it's already one of the most powerful tools we've ever built. And while it's true that AI can amplify the trap, it can also do something else. When used well, AI can become a thinking partner, helping us stretch the way we see, ask, imagine and decide.

But only if we've done the thinking first.

AI is brilliant at expanding, not clarifying. It can multiply your momentum, but it can't choose the direction or sense whether something is meaningful. That's still our job. Once that job is done however, and the real question is clear, what AI can help us do becomes extraordinary.

But what does that look like in practice?

In medicine, researchers at MIT have used AI models trained on non-biological datasets to identify entirely new antibiotics - compounds no human would've found on their own. The AI didn't replace expertise; it challenged the way we search, surfacing novel possibilities that had been overlooked.

In architecture, generative AI is helping designers simulate how buildings respond to light, wind and temperature. These factors once took months of modelling to understand. This is not skipping the creative process. It involves adding layers of insight the human brain alone can't map. The result? Structures that are both beautiful and radically energy-efficient that are designed using a kind of human–machine co-thinking.

In conservation, AI models are being trained to detect illegal deforestation from satellite data, faster than any human team ever could. But the real innovation wasn't the algorithm. It was the mindset of the people who asked: 'What if we could intervene before it's too late?' The system wasn't just efficient. It was human thinking, extended by machine patterning, applied with urgency.

These are just a few of countless examples that show what becomes possible when we don't hand over our thinking to AI but instead, invite it to extend it.

When we reclaim our own thinking, AI becomes
something else entirely. Not a shortcut, but a multiplier.

So far in this chapter, we've focused on what becomes possible when individual thinking can break free of The Answer Trap and how that enables us to tap into the opportunities of AI.

Now, let's widen our perspective and explore what becomes possible when groups and societies also take back cognitive control.

Most groups don't realise they're stuck until the signs become visible: fatigue, frustration, or failure to follow through. But once they see the trap, the real question becomes, 'what shifts when they break free?'

That's where things get interesting.

THE HIDDEN COST OF FRICTION

Have you ever thought about how much energy gets wasted managing the hidden friction in groups when they're trying to get stuff done?

It's not just the big clashes, but all the little disconnects. The constant need for clarification, the sideways glances, the second-guessing. That kind of environment is utterly exhausting.

Even the best teams feel this. They might not be dysfunctional, but they're definitely tired. Tired from translating their thinking and from chasing clarity that never quite sticks. And, they're tired from trying to stay aligned while the goalposts keep changing.

That's a huge drain on collective energy.

However, when a group learns to truly think together, that whole dynamic starts to shift. Friction eases, not always instantly, but enough to feel a real difference. Conversations flow more smoothly. People stop guarding their own patch and start engaging with what's happening around them. The emotional load lightens and the effort required to keep things on track starts to drop.

As that weight lifts, energy comes flooding back.

Groups that learn to think together don't just reduce friction; they unlock a powerful sense of intellectual and emotional momentum. They free up capacity that was being burned on things that didn't need to be so hard.

In today's complex world, that regained capacity is gold.

WHAT THINKING TOGETHER REALLY MEANS

Thinking together doesn't mean everyone agrees, sees things the same way or holds back to keep things smooth. It means people are willing to think things through in real time, to stay with a question longer than feels comfortable and pause long enough to test whether they're actually aligned.

When this happens, the conversation can focus on the things that are important, instead of trying to work out where everyone else is coming from.

In these moments, difference and diverse perspectives become useful. Not a source of conflict or confusion, but a spark for better thinking.

Groups don't have to collapse around the fastest answer because they've built the cohesive understanding beneath it. They stop working in parallel and start building shared momentum that holds, because it's anchored in something the group created together.

When disruption hits, that foundation matters. Why?

Because groups that take the time to build cognitive alignment can adapt together. They know what is important (and what isn't) and can adjust and find a new way forward without needing to reset every time a planned path is disrupted.

In short, they adapt faster. They're focused instead of fragmented. And most importantly, they're flexible because they're able to move with freedom within a shared framework.

HOW SHARED CLARITY TRANSFORMS

One of the most overlooked benefits of thinking together - and avoiding The Answer Trap's pitfalls - is that it makes collaboration scalable. Not just easier, but sustainable, no matter where people are located.

When a group takes the time to align on what truly matters, not just what's next, they create something more powerful than a plan.

> *It's a mental map. One that provides a shared point of reference, helps people quickly work out where they are, shows the hazards to avoid and makes it clear why something is, or is not, important.*

In my work with teams, I call this mental map The Vital Thread[1]. It's like the emergency lights on the floor of an aircraft. The ones you don't think about until the cabin goes dark. It doesn't tell you exactly what to do, but it shows you how to move when the pressure's on.

The Vital Thread isn't a policy, a process or a checklist. It's a shared string of logic that runs through every conversation, every decision and every moment that matters. Once it's in place, the group doesn't need constant catchups to stay on track.

Further, when a Vital Thread sits beneath any strategy, the thinking travels with the work. It provides an understanding of the *why*, not just the *what*. This allows people to keep collaborating, even when they're not in the same room, the same meeting or the same time zone. And, no matter how many people there are.

One performing arts organisation I worked with built their Vital Thread just months before the COVID pandemic hit. When most of their revenue stream disappeared overnight, they didn't freeze. They used that thread to make decisions quickly and clearly. What to pause, what to protect and where to adapt. The answers weren't easy, but they made sense. Most importantly, the organisation made it through.

---

1. If you're curious to learn more about The Vital Thread I discuss it in significant detail in my book The Thrive Cycle (2016).

'The Vital Thread became our anchor,' my client told me later. 'When everything else felt impossible, it gave us a way to move. It didn't tell us what to do but it gave us a way to work it out quickly, consistently and collaboratively - even when we were all working from home.'

If a single thread can hold a team together through a crisis, what happens when no thread exists at all? That's the reality in many systems, where The Answer Trap is not just common. It's entrenched.

THE COURAGE TO BE UNCOMFORTABLE

It was 2015 and the official answer was already in. Was the water in Flint, Michigan, safe?

'Yes'.

At least that's what the city, the state and the US Environmental Protection Agency said. Sure, there were issues, but the prevailing view was that it was under control. No further action needed.

Dr Mona Hanna-Attisha, a paediatrician seeing children in the community, didn't agree. She noticed something alarming: lead levels in children were rising sharply after the city changed its water source. She listened to parents, looked at the data and did something the system wasn't doing.

She stayed with the question. Not just 'Is this bad?' but 'What are we not seeing?' 'Why doesn't this add up?' 'What are we trying not to know?'

She went public with her findings and was immediately dismissed, discredited, told she didn't understand the full picture. And she kept going. Because the goal wasn't just to *be* right; it was to keep the question alive long enough for the truth to be seen.

And eventually, it was.

The system shifted under the weight of evidence and public pressure. The water source was changed back. Federal investigations began and people paid attention. Not because she had presented a perfect solution from day one, but because she refused to stop thinking and questioning when everyone else had already moved on to the accepted answer.

Fifteen-year-old Greta Thunberg did something similar on a global stage.

While politicians debated incremental targets and complex timelines for climate action, she asked a simpler, more fundamental question: If we *know* the science is urgent, why aren't we acting like it?

She didn't arrive with a polished press release or stand at an official podium initially; she showed up with a handwritten sign and a willingness to sit in the discomfort that many others wanted to move past. She didn't offer the perfect answer. She held on to the real question. And, when enough people stopped long enough to *think together* with her, that question got harder and harder to ignore.

That's the power of staying with the question and resisting *The Answer Trap*. Not because it's easy but because it's often the only thing that shifts what's possible, especially in systems that are wired to reach for closure and resist fundamental challenges.

MAKE IT REAL

Take some time to think about The Answer Trap and where it shows up in your world. At work, home, in your family or anywhere else.

What does it look like?

_____

_____

What impact is the trap having today?

_____

_____

What could breaking free look like?

_____

_____

What would that mean for you and those involved?

_____

_____

Key takeaway:

To fall into The Answer Trap is human. To break free? That is a choice.

RECLAIMING CONTROL

Imagine what would be possible if there were more of these moments – in communities, in institutions or in entire countries. Systems don't break themselves free of The Answer Trap; they tend to reinforce it.

It's individuals who break free first. People who notice the pattern, who resist the rush for easy answers and stay with the uncomfortable question longer than the world around them is comfortable with.

And that's where we go next.

Before you can shift a team, a system or a culture, you have to know how to shift yourself. Part 2 is about what's happening in your head, in real time.

This is where we stop talking about *what* The Answer Trap *is* and start talking about how it works *on you*.

CHAPTER IN A NUTSHELL

- Breaking free of The Answer Trap doesn't give you instant certainty - it gives you space: to think, to notice and to lead with clarity.

- Clarity feels like a slow exhale, not a lightning bolt. It quietens urgency and makes room for what actually matters.

- AI can accelerate the trap - or extend your thinking - but only if you're asking the right question to begin with.

- When groups escape the trap, they stop working in parallel and start thinking together - building shared logic, not just shared plans.

- Alignment isn't agreement. True momentum comes from pausing long enough to check if we're talking about, let alone solving, the same problem.

- Clarity reduces hidden friction and restores energy - making collaboration more scalable, adaptive and human.

- Systems don't free themselves. People do - by staying with the question, long enough to shift what's possible.

PART 2:

MAKE THE
SWITCH

**FLIP
THE LID**

**SPOT YOUR
DEFAULT**

**SHIFT TO
COPILOT**

PART 2: WHAT TO EXPECT

You saw The Answer Trap in action, felt its pull, understood its escalating costs and recognised how even powerful tools like AI can accelerate our drift into default responses. You also gained a glimpse of what's possible when you break free.

So, by now you know *what* the trap is and *why* escaping it matters.

But simply seeing the pattern often isn't enough to change it, especially when pressure mounts.

Why do we keep falling into the same reactive thinking patterns, even when we know better? And, what's happening beneath the surface, in our own cognitive wiring, that makes the pull of premature closure so strong?

That deep dive into the mechanics of our own minds is the core focus of Part 2. Here, we move beyond identifying the trap to understanding the internal systems that make us vulnerable to it.

Over the next five chapters we'll lift the lid on our everyday thinking and delve into this hidden world.

We'll discover how the core issue lies in *how you think*, not just *what you do* and reveal the underlying cognitive system your brain uses every day, including the different thinking modes that get thrown off course by disruption.

You'll diagnose your own rapid-fire reaction when pressure hits and gain clarity on this pattern by meeting the five Cognitive Autopilots.

To bring it all together, you'll see these Autopilots collide in a real-world scenario, exposing how individual defaults fuel collective drift.

Part 2 equips you with three crucial pieces: a deep understanding of the cognitive mechanics behind your reactions, what your specific thinking habit is and how it pulls you into The Answer Trap.

I promise. You'll never think about thinking the same way again.

So, let's take a look.

CHAPTER 6
THE THINKING PROBLEM

You now know about The Answer Trap. You've seen it and you've felt it. You recognise it in yourself and you spot it in others.

And that's the funny thing.

Most people go through life oblivious to its existence. It's kind of like *the matrix*, from the original 1999 movie of the same name. Once you know it's there you can't unsee it.

The Answer Trap is everywhere.

Alas, awareness isn't enough. That realisation can be unsettling. It raises the one question sitting just beneath the surface.

How do I break free?

This is exactly the kind of situation where The Answer Trap tightens its grip.

If I told you I had a three-step formula that guaranteed you'd never fall into the trap again, part of you would probably want to hear it.

Of course it would.

Your brain craves the clarity of a plan, the certainty of a solution and the relief of feeling like you're back in control.

I could give you that formula. In fact, I could give you ten of them. Each one might work some of the time, in some situations. But none of them would set you free. Why?

Because The Answer Trap isn't an action problem.
It's a thinking problem.

NOT THE WRONG ACTION, THE WRONG PATTERN

When people feel stuck, they often assume the antidote is to *do* more. So, they intensify the effort. They push harder, gather more data and make faster decisions, believing that effort and momentum will eventually break the deadlock.

The Answer Trap isn't caused by a lack of action. It's caused by the underlying thinking that drives the action, especially under pressure.

We don't fall into the trap because we're lazy or unclear.

*We fall because our brain is running too fast to stop
and ask what kind of thinking the moment really
needs.*

Consequently, it grabs the familiar thinking habit, the one that usually works and feels like control. It doesn't check whether the situation is clear, or whether the job that needs to be done is different from last time.

Our brain defaults. Then, it starts running.

From the outside, the activity still looks like progress. That's what makes the trap so hard to catch. Tasks get done, meetings move forward and lists or plans get written. However, what's missing is the clarity that holds everything together.

It's not absent because no one's thinking. Quite the contrary.

*It's missing because everyone's locked into their own
version of thinking. The one their brain believes the
situation requires.*

It's like a repetitive, unconscious loop. Unless we notice it and deliberately break free, we stay trapped within it. Acting, adjusting, delivering, yet all without ever asking whether the answer we're chasing is still the one that's needed.

WHAT YOUR BRAIN IS REALLY TRYING TO PROTECT

Here's the part many people miss.

When disruption hits, your brain isn't focused solely on the task in front of you. It's focused on what that task is meant to deliver: the underlying job it's trying to complete beneath the surface. That job might be achieving momentum, clarity, control, purpose, progress, connection or even just a moment of relief.

Most of the time, that system works well. The task gets done, the job feels complete and your brain moves on, quietly satisfied that things are heading in the right direction.

But when disruption scrambles the task or blocks the path, something shifts. The job suddenly feels harder to complete. The underlying need, no matter what it is, starts to feel at risk. And that's when your brain steps in to protect you. It's not a failure or a lack of discipline. It's a survival response.

Here's where the trap is set.

Once that protective loop kicks in, your brain doesn't stop to ask, 'What's the job now?' It just reacts, grabbing the fastest thinking pattern it knows to make the discomfort stop. That might involve pushing forward, pulling back, tightening the detail, chasing the next idea or trying to hold everything together. It's doing what it knows works. Or at least, what has worked in the past.

That's how you can feel busy, responsive and engaged yet still be completely off track.

Your brain is trying to protect the need but, in its urgency, it locks onto the wrong job.

Now, some of this may sound a little conceptual at this point. If you're finding this to be the case, don't worry. In a while, we'll step through some tangible examples to show exactly what's going on.

WHY YOUR BRAIN DOES WHAT IT DOES

Most of the time, thinking just happens. You don't plan it or map it out. You just start moving, focused on the task, the decision and the outcome. It feels instinctive. Natural even. Like you're simply responding to what's in front of you.

Beneath the surface, your brain is doing far more than it seems.

It's scanning the situation and weighing up what's at stake. It chooses a thinking pattern based on what it assumes the situation requires.

Often, it gets it right. Sometimes, however, it doesn't. When that happens, we don't just stall; we drift, react or focus on the wrong thing.

That's where a concept that I call *cognitive mechanics* can be helpful.

It refers to the internal systems that shape how you think, decide and respond under pressure. They influence which thinking mode your brain defaults to, how quickly you react and whether your thinking adapts, or repeats the same unhelpful loop.

Most of these systems run invisibly, yet they don't have to. This is where we start to take back control. Why?

When you can see how your thinking works, you can engage with it. If you can engage with it, you can shift it. And when you can shift it, you're no longer stuck in reactive thinking.

That's what this next part is about. Not fixing your thinking or following a new rulebook. Its goal is to help you engage your brain in a new way. It flips the lid (like lifting the bonnet of a car to reveal the engine) enabling you to see your own cognitive mechanics clearly and start making different moves when it matters most.

WHERE WE'RE GOING NEXT

This is where it gets personal.

It's one thing to understand the problem ie. to 'get it' intellectually. It's quite another to see how it shows up in you.

The next few chapters are designed to do exactly that. Not through tips or tricks, but by helping you recognise the fast, protective thinking patterns that quietly take over when the moment gets messy.

You'll start to see your own defaults and your own protective cognitive loops. The goal is not to judge them, but to understand why they exist and how they shape the way you lead, decide and respond, both at work and in life.

Here is where real change starts.

CHAPTER IN A NUTSHELL

- We don't get stuck because we're not acting; we get stuck because we're not thinking in the way the moment requires.

- Under pressure, our brain protects what it believes we're losing: progress, control, clarity, connection – something we want and value.

- That protection kicks in before we realise it, triggering fast loops or thinking patterns that feel like thinking but often lock us into the wrong job.

- These loops aren't flaws; they're part of how our thinking system works.

- Once we can see those patterns, we can begin to change the way we engage our brain and actively influence our thinking, not just our actions.

CHAPTER 7

WHAT FIRES FIRST?

This chapter is different. You're here to notice something about yourself.

In the next few pages, you'll step into a high-pressure moment. One where something you care about feels at risk. And what we're paying attention to is the very first move your brain makes.

It's not about what you think you should do or what you'd do after a deep breath and a whiteboard session. We're looking for the move that fires before you even realise it's happening.

By the end of this chapter, you'll have seen that first move.

Resist the rip

There's a brief window, right before your brain steps in, when you get a clear look at what's really going on in your thinking. It's raw, unfiltered and it doesn't last long.

That's because your brain is wired to protect you. The second it senses discomfort, it starts smoothing things over and trying to make the situation feel more manageable or familiar.

The first time you see your default thinking pattern is the clearest. After that, your brain starts editing the story.

So, before you read on, pause and give yourself ten quiet minutes. The more space you create for the next few pages, the more you'll notice and the more you'll get out of the book.

Resist the classic Answer Trap move, flipping over the pages to see what's coming up.

You may not feel 'the rip' now, but trust me, in about 30 seconds you definitely will. So, this is your opportunity to notice it, then choose to do something different.

We're about to catch something your brain usually skips over, so you won't want to miss it.

WHERE IT ALL STARTS

Most people focus on what to *do* next when pressure hits. The decision, the action or the plan. But what really shapes the outcome happens just before that.

It's the flicker. A fast, protective move your brain makes the moment something you care about feels at risk.

It happens quickly, often before you've noticed. And once it kicks in, it starts shaping how you see the situation, what you focus on, and the kind of answer your brain will chase. This is what we're about to surface.

Okay.

Ready?

Let's make this real.

FEEL THE MOMENT

Imagine that your phone rings. You take the call.

Finally, you've been given that once in a career opportunity you've been waiting for. It's the kind that could define your reputation, or damage it if it goes wrong.

The brief is vague, the deadline's tight, and the politics are already humming underneath.

It's complex and you're relying on people to deliver. Many you don't know, some you don't like, and others you definitely don't trust.

The pressure hits faster than you expect. You hang up the phone and you instantly feel it.

Your stomach drops. Chest tightens. Mind goes blank.

But just underneath it, something else kicks in. An urge. A reflex. A move.

At first, you might not notice it. It's fast. Subtle, but powerful. What fires in your brain in that moment is already shaping what happens next.

So, stay with it and notice what's happening.

It might be a thought or a reaction that feels like taking control.

On the following page are five responses – from A to E. They all make sense under pressure, but one, will feel more like you than the others.

Read them.

Feel them.

Pick the one that lands first.

WHAT FIRES FIRST?

Which of the following resonates most with you?

A	OK, what's the next move? We can't stall now. If I don't push this forward, we'll get stuck. - *I move quickly because staying still feels like we're losing.*
B	Wait, do we even have enough to move yet? This could go wrong quickly if we don't get it right now. - *I scan for gaps because if we miss something, we'll pay for it later.*
C	Is this even the right approach? There's got to be a smarter way. This brief is too narrow; we're solving the wrong problem. - *I challenge the thinking because possibility always feels worth chasing.*
D	We haven't even started, and I can already feel people pulling in different directions. If we don't align first, I'll have to hold everything together. - *I sense the drift early because holding the group together is what keeps us moving.*
E	This is already messy; if we don't clean it up, we'll mess it up. If we rush this, we'll regret it later. - *I tighten things fast because if it's not sharp, it won't hold.*

WHAT'S YOUR BACKUP MOVE?

Okay. So, now you have your first reaction. What if you couldn't respond in that first way?

Which of the statements would be the next most like you?

[✓]	A	B	C	D	E
1st choice					
2nd choice					

WHAT THAT REACTION TELLS YOU

What you just picked wasn't random. It wasn't personality, nor was it about your level of experience or competence. It was your Autopilot — the fast-thinking cognitive pattern your brain runs when things are unclear and the pressure rises.

The moment something you cared about felt at risk, your brain didn't stop to analyse. It did what it's wired to do: grab the move that feels like it will steady you and chase what restores control, momentum, certainty or clarity.

And that instinct? It's smart and protective. It's designed to get you moving when things get messy.

But there's a catch.

That Autopilot loop doesn't check if it's right for *this* moment. It just runs. And once it's running, it shapes everything:

- How you see the situation

- What you define as the problem
- What options you even notice
- The answer you chase, often too quickly

That's how smart people, good thinkers, get pulled straight into The Answer Trap.

WHERE WE GO NEXT

Soon, you'll meet your Autopilot properly, but first, we need to zoom out. Why?

Because your Autopilot doesn't run in isolation. It's part of a system your brain relies on every day to get things done. That system is designed to help you move toward what matters and avoid what doesn't.

Spotting your default thinking pattern without understanding that system is like zooming in on one part of a photo. It might look clear, even familiar, but without the full picture you can't see what you're really looking at. Consequently, you risk misreading it or reacting to the wrong thing entirely.

So, once again, I encourage you to resist the rip. Don't flip over the chapters and let The Answer Trap win.

And, yes, in case you're wondering… this *is* a test.

- *Will you choose to stay with the discomfort of not knowing your Autopilot or seek premature closure?*

Okay. With that out of the way, let's take a closer look at how that system behaves and what happens when disruption throws it off course.

Stay with me. It will be worth it.

CHAPTER 8
EVERYDAY THINKING

How often do you think about why you're doing something?

Most of the time when we act, we're just trying to get something done that matters. We don't take on tasks for the sake of it; there's always something we need or want underneath.

The instant we wake up, our brain gets to work. Quietly, automatically, it starts moving toward something better. We might be seeking more productivity, progress or purpose. Perhaps we want more enjoyment, control or connection. Often, we're trying to achieve less frustration, stagnation or isolation.

Some of these underlying needs driving our actions are easy to spot.

We work to earn a living. Yet underneath that, we're also seeking productivity: the sense that we're contributing and progressing. We're also chasing control.

For instance, over our choices, our time and our future.

We cook dinner because our body needs food. That's true, but it's not just about nutrition. It can also give us a sense of progress (something ticked off the list), control (a predictable outcome), or even pleasure (comfort, creativity or caring for others and ourselves).

We learn new skills, often in pursuit of something more than knowledge. We're looking for purpose, growth or progress. We want to feel like we're moving forward rather than standing still.

Other needs are harder to name, but just as powerful.

We organise a catch up with friends, not just for fun, but perhaps because we're craving connection. We pick up a hobby, hoping to spark creativity or bring a little meaning back into our routine. We wrestle with a hard decision, because deep down, we're trying to feel more in control of what happens next or reduce the risk.

These aren't just abstract ideas; they are fundamental needs that quietly shape our daily lives. When we feel a lack of productivity in our work, or a slowdown in our personal progress, or perhaps a missing sense of purpose in our routines, our brain registers this as a 'gap.'

Similarly, a craving for pleasure, a desire for more perceived control, or a yearning for personal connection can all initiate a cascade of actions. These underlying needs act as the compass points for our brains, constantly nudging us toward situations that promise to fulfill them.

GETTING FROM A TO B: THE REAL REASON WE TAKE ACTION

At any given moment, there's a gap between where we are and where we want to be. I call it the A to B gap.

Point A is our current state. It might be messy, uncomfortable or simply not enough. **Point B** is the desired state. It's the place where things feel better, clearer or more in control.

The bigger the gap is, and the more important the outcome feels, the harder our brain works to close it. This is especially true when something we care about is at risk.

Imagine this.

It's a workday and you've got a big presentation to give. You've just woken up, tired and groggy. Right now, you're at Point A. But you need to be at Point B: alert, energised and ready to perform.

Why do you care? Because there are deeper needs at stake. For instance, protecting your credibility, avoiding embarrassment, or feeling competent and in control. Your reputation is at stake.

If you're groggy before a high-stakes presentation, those needs feel at risk. So, your brain kicks into gear because it wants to protect you. The bigger the gap and the more important the need, the harder your brain works to close it.

This drives action. A task. In this instance, you take a cold shower. This is your brain's way of helping you close the gap between A and B to get the job of protecting your needs done.

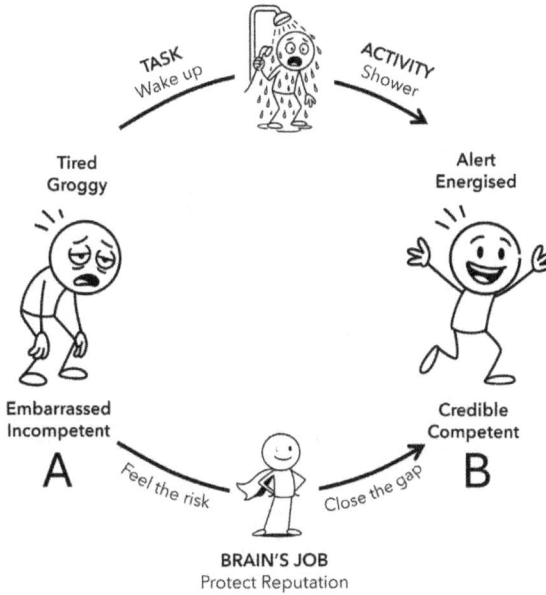

TASK
Wake up

ACTIVITY
Shower

Tired
Groggy

Alert
Energised

Embarrassed
Incompetent

A

Credible
Competent

B

Feel the risk

Close the gap

BRAIN'S JOB
Protect Reputation

But why am I raising any of this?

Under everyday circumstances your brain doesn't just launch into one big task. It uses different modes of thinking. Each is designed to help you get a specific kind of job done.

If we're going to escape The Answer Trap by choosing deliberate over default thinking, we first need something important.

We need to understand how thinking works. So, let's flip the lid and go a little deeper.

HOW WE GET THERE: YOUR BRAIN'S THINKING MODES

To get these jobs done, your brain shifts between different modes of thinking. This usually isn't a conscious choice; it happens because your brain is wired to help you close the A to B gap, moving from where you are now to where you want to be, as quickly and easily as possible.

Each mode plays a different role in navigating the world and accomplishing your underlying jobs.

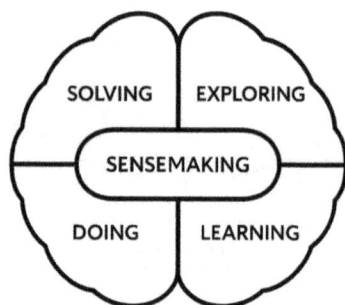

One mode is **Doing**. Here, you simply act. Your brain sees a clear task and gets on with it. This is the mode for executing known steps, getting things done, ticking items off the list and moving forward efficiently.

Another mode is **Solving**. In this mode, you focus intently. Your brain zooms in on a specific problem, trying to fix what's broken, overcome an obstacle or figure out what's getting in the way of progress.

Then there's **Learning** mode. Here, you scan your environment or your knowledge. You start looking for what's missing, asking questions, gathering information, seeking expertise or filling in gaps in your understanding.

Exploring mode is different again. Here, you stretch your thinking. Your brain opens up, playing with possibilities, brainstorming alternatives, testing new angles and wondering what else could work beyond the obvious solutions.

Finally, there's **Sensemaking** mode. In this mode, you check in and reflect. You pause to consider what's shifted, what you've learned from recent experiences, what patterns are emerging and what really matters now in the bigger picture.

These modes aren't a checklist or a strict sequence. Your brain doesn't methodically move through them in a predefined order. It just picks the mode that seems most useful for making progress, based on the situation and the need your brain is trying to protect.

THINKING MODES IN MOTION: THE COFFEE EXAMPLE

Even something as simple as getting a coffee shows how naturally your brain moves between different thinking modes, potentially all in just a few minutes.

Let's continue the day we started earlier.

You've now made it to your workplace and decided that the cold shower wasn't quite enough to get you ready for that big presentation. So, you decide to go and buy a coffee.

Your brain might start in **Doing** mode: you walk into your regular café and order your usual flat white. No intentional thought. No decision. Just habit.

Then you pause. You remember how little you slept. Your brain shifts briefly into **Solving** mode: *'Maybe I need a double shot today.'*

The job hasn't changed. You still need to feel alert and ready. But your brain is adjusting the task based on your current state. It's still working to protect what matters (in this case, being sharp for what's ahead), but the mode shifts to help you match the situation.

Perhaps you enter **Learning** mode when you ask the barista, 'What's the difference between oat and almond milk anyway?' You're filling in a knowledge gap so you can make a better choice next time.

Maybe you switch into **Exploring** mode as you glance at the menu and wonder, 'What haven't I tried before?' You're not solving a problem here; you're playing with possibilities and novelty.

And finally, you might engage **Sensemaking** mode as you take a sip and pause to reflect, 'Do I actually feel more awake now?' You're checking in, evaluating the outcome and seeing whether the job is done.

Your brain's just doing what it's built to do: pick the fastest, easiest way to get the job done. Whether the job is simple or complex, that adaptive system usually works quite well.

But what happens when a task no longer works, when the usual path to Point B is blocked?

WHEN DISRUPTION HITS

Instead of the coffee scenario, let's bring things closer to home. Imagine you're a parent with three school-aged children.

It's a regular weekday morning. You wake up and the tasks are pre-set. They're the same ones you do every day. Have breakfast, help get the kids dressed, throw lunches together and get everyone out the door by 8:15am.

It's a standard routine with no big decisions and no overthinking. You're in *Doing* mode and it works. The tasks are known and the job is clear: get the day started with a sense of calm, control and connection. Why?

Because in your mind, that's what being a good parent is all about.

The four types of disruption

The system works. Your finely tuned cognitive mechanics are functioning like a well-oiled machine. Each part does exactly what it needs to, without conscious effort.

However, disruption changes this. And yet, not all disruption is the same and nor does it test the same part of your brain.

There are four types.

- *Activity disruption* affects *how* you do something.

  The job and task are still clear; you just need a different method. There's no bread, so you toast something else. Same task, same outcome but the activity changes. Your brain flickers into *Solving* then back into *Doing* mode and adjusts easily.

- *Task disruption* affects *what* you do.

  Maybe the car won't start so you decide to catch the bus instead. The job stays the same, get the kids to school, but the task changes. You shift into *Solving* mode then switch to a new task, catching the bus. There's a bit more stress, but your brain is still able to manage.

- *Pattern disruption* happens when the whole routine breaks down.

  The kids are tired. You're tired and nothing is landing. The job hasn't changed, you're still trying to get everyone out the door, but none of the tasks are working the way they should.

  To be effective, your brain needs to move beyond *Doing* and *Solving*. It needs to pause, observe and shift into *Sensemaking*. But under pressure, that doesn't always happen. Instead, you intensify the energy and urgency behind the tasks. More rushing. More snapping.

Now, the fourth type of disruption runs deeper. Let's stay with the parenting example but this time, push it further.

Imagine it's been weeks of tension. The kids are withdrawn, and mornings are increasingly fraught with everyone on edge.

You've tried everything: better routines, calmer tone, getting up earlier, being more flexible, even applying stricter rules. Some things work for a day or two, then fall apart.

One morning, your youngest refuses to get dressed. Another starts crying in the car. You ask what's wrong, and the older one says:

'I don't know. Everything just feels bad.'

You feel it too. The routine no longer helps and none of the usual strategies land. The energy in the house has shifted and you can't pin down what changed or why.

Is it school pressure? Something online? A health issue? Is it me? All of the above? None of them?

Suddenly, it's not just about being a good parent. You're not even sure what 'good' looks like right now or where you would even begin to work it out.

The problem feels too ambiguous to name and too slippery to fix. And yet the mornings keep coming and the challenges keep building.

This is Type 4: *Cumulative disruption.*

It's not just one event or one task failing. It's disruption layered on disruption, without space to recover or reset.

You keep adapting, but nothing sticks. The thinking modes that usually help you close the gap between A and B can't land anymore. The target keeps shifting and the rules keep changing.

Of course, Cumulative disruption isn't limited to morning routines at home.

It happens at work too.

You're leading a team through yet another change. There are new priorities, shifting reporting lines and another urgent project just kicked off. You've already restructured the workflow twice, adjusted roles and recruited new people, but the context keeps changing. One day it's budget pressure and the next, a rebrand. Then, someone resigns.

Every time you try to stabilise things, something else moves. You start to wonder:

> *What's the actual job now? Is it delivery? Alignment? Morale? Survival?*

The answer keeps changing and that's the problem.

Your brain is working overtime trying to engage the mode of thinking you need but the system that has historically made humans successful now struggles.

There's no stable frame of reference, problems don't have single causes, and they are fuzzy around the edges. There are also less clearcut solutions and fewer ways to tell what's working and what's not.

THE DRIFT INTO AUTOPILOT

Whether we're at work or home, Cumulative disruption in the world is increasing rapidly.

When the underlying job is unclear, the usual tasks don't work and the gap between A and B feels too big to close, your brain doesn't always stop and calmly reassess. It keeps trying to protect what matters in the most efficient way it can.

Instead of moving seamlessly between the different thinking modes based on what the situation needs, your brain grabs what's familiar. Namely, the pattern of thinking that feels safest or most instinctive under pressure. It's the one it trusts because it has worked in the past.

That's when your Autopilot kicks in.

Not because you've stopped caring, but because you care so much and your brain just wants the discomfort of being stuck between A and B to end.

So, let's dive into the next chapter, where you'll meet your Autopilot and discover how it lures your thinking into The Answer Trap.

CHAPTER IN A NUTSHELL

- Every task we take on is driven by a deeper job: getting something we want more of, or avoiding something we want less of.

- Our brain is wired to close the gap between where we are (Point A) and where we want to be (Point B) as quickly and efficiently as possible.

- To do this, it shifts between different thinking modes: Doing, Solving, Learning, Exploring and Sensemaking.

- These modes often operate automatically in the background, helping us get things done until disruption throws them off course.

- Not all disruption impacts our thinking in the same way. There are four types: activity, task, pattern and cumulative.

- That's when the system stalls. Not because we've stopped thinking, but because we're using the wrong kind of thinking for the situation at hand.

- When our brain feels stuck between points A and B, it defaults to the thinking pattern that feels familiar. It hands over the controls to Autopilot.

CHAPTER 9

WHEN YOUR AUTOPILOT TAKES OVER

In the last chapter, we explored what happens to your thinking when the world gets messy. You saw how your brain moves through different modes (doing, solving, learning, exploring and sensemaking) to get important jobs done.

But in disruption, that system starts to buckle and that's when your default thinking begins. It doesn't announce itself. It just quietly takes the wheel and starts doing what it's always done: protecting what matters most. Namely, your needs and the sense that you're still progressing from A to B.

This thinking pattern feels automatic. Natural, like you're doing exactly what's needed. Sometimes you are, but other times, that instinctive loop keeps you locked in motion, focusing on the thing that feels most uncomfortable, not the one that actually matters.

I call this your *Cognitive Autopilot*. In this chapter, you're going to meet yours.

RECONNECT TO YOUR DIAGNOSTIC

Do you remember, back in Chapter 7, I asked you to choose the set of statements (A through E) that felt most like you?

It offered a way to surface your instinct: how your brain responds when things feel uncertain or at risk.

Maybe one option stood out. Or maybe it shifted depending on the stakes or who else was in the room. Either way, your response wasn't random. Each set reflected a distinct Autopilot, a default thinking pattern your brain turns to when something important is on the line.

This isn't a label or a box. It's simply a reflection of how your brain protects what matters. Efficiently, automatically and often without you even realising it.

Psychologist Robert Sternberg once said that intelligence isn't about logic, it's about choosing the right kind of thinking for the moment. That's what these patterns reveal. Each one is your brain's way of choosing the kind of thinking it trusts most, especially when the pressure's on.

THE FIVE AUTOPILOTS

For decades, psychologists have studied how human thinking patterns shift under pressure, especially when uncertainty threatens something we care about. The five Cognitive Autopilots you're about to explore are grounded in that research and shaped by re-al-world patterns I've seen again and again[2].

Each Autopilot is driven by a deep, often unconscious belief your brain holds about how to stay safe when things feel complex and uncertain. While we all draw on all five at different times, one or two usually rise to the surface when the pressure hits.

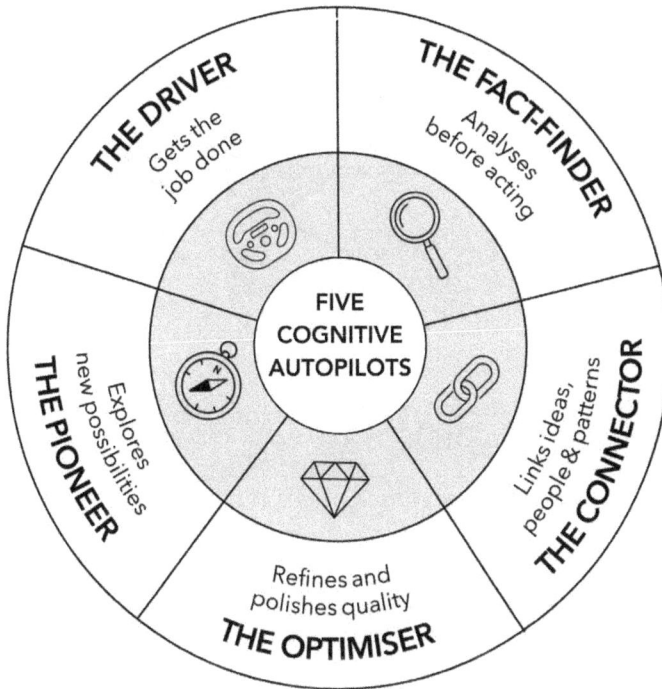

If you haven't already, flick back to Chapter 7 and remind yourself which set of statements resonated most with you. That was your instinct speaking.

---

2. Discover the research behind the Autopilots in the Further Reading and References section at the back of the book.

Now's your chance to understand those patterns more clearly, starting with the one your brain tends to reach for first. Each description is intentionally detailed, designed to help you spot the signs in yourself and others.

I suggest beginning by reading the two Autopilots that felt most familiar for you, then circle back to the others.

The Driver Autopilot: When action feels like safety

If you chose **Option A**, you've already met the Driver. Even if you didn't have a name for it yet. The statements were:

- OK, what's the next move? We can't stall now.
- If I don't push this forward, we'll get stuck.
- I move quickly because staying still feels like we're losing.

This is the Driver at work. The Autopilot that equates movement with control.

When things feel messy or stalled, you don't freeze.
You step in. You act, because standing still feels like
giving up ground.

Psychologists have found that when uncertainty strikes, the brain often speeds up. Not because the path is clear, but because action feels like protection. The Driver thinking pattern lives in that instinct.

If this resonates, the following might sound familiar.

You're in a team conversation and it's stuck, going back-and-forth. Around and around the discussion goes. People hesitate. Then, something in your brain fires: *Let's just decide. We need to move.*

For the Driver, the perceived risk isn't getting it wrong. It's getting stuck. Action feels like progress and momentum feels like safety.

That instinct can be powerful. The Driver gets things done by cutting through the noise and pushing forward when others stall.

You might recognise this Autopilot if you've thought:

- We just need to act. Any decision is better than none.
- Let's move. We can fix it later.
- I'm not letting this stall. I'll drive it myself if I have to.

You're not responding to the situation.
You're trying to outrun it.

When this Autopilot takes over, you keep chasing movement because stopping feels dangerous. But in the rush to move, it's easy to forget to ask: *Are we even running the right race?*

Have you ever shut down a family discussion with *'Fine, we're getting takeaway. I'm done'*? Or pushed a team to sign off early *'because we need to land something'* even if it wasn't quite right?

That's your Driver at work.

It's not trying to dominate, just trying to protect you by keeping things moving.

The Fact-Finder Autopilot: When knowing feels like safety

If **Option B** felt familiar, then the Fact-Finder is probably a pattern you know well. Its statements were:

- Wait, do we even have enough to move yet?
- This could go wrong fast if we don't get it right.
- I scan for gaps because if we miss something, we'll pay for it later.

It's the Autopilot that reaches for certainty when things feel unclear. It means that you don't rush in; you scan, check and dig.

Moving forward without the full picture feels risky. And risk, for the Fact-Finder, feels like failure waiting to happen.

Neuroscience shows that uncertainty triggers the same part of the brain as physical pain. It makes sense, then, that your instinct is to fill the gaps; information becomes your shield. The Fact-Finder doesn't seek control through action, but through understanding.

Imagine that a decision's looming and that the stakes are high. There are a lot of unknowns, so your brain locks in: *'Just one more check. One more detail. Then I'll be ready.'* The Fact-Finder doesn't freeze, it scans then gathers.

It slows things down, not to avoid the decision, but to protect the outcome.

That instinct can be gold. The Fact-Finder spots what others miss. It sees the blind spots, strengthens the logic and prevents costly mistakes.

You might recognise this thinking loop if you've thought:

- I just need to know a bit more before we decide.
- What if we've missed something critical?
- Let me double check that; we can't risk the wrong call.

You're not trying to delay the decision. You're trying to make sure it's the right one.

What your brain is protecting is certainty, control over the risk and the belief that getting it right means focusing intently on not getting it wrong.

When this Autopilot takes over, you start collecting information to feel ready, but the decision doesn't necessarily get any clearer. You're trying to ease the discomfort of uncertainty with more data, but no amount of information will make the moment feel completely safe.

Eventually, the window for action quietly closes.

Has this ever happened to you?

You've spent hours comparing options for a basic purchase because you think 'what if I pick the wrong one?' Or you've asked one more clarifying question in a meeting, not because it would change the decision, but because acting still felt too soon.

That's your Fact-Finder at work.

It's not trying to stall, just trying to protect you by making sure you're ready.

The Pioneer Autopilot: When new feels like safety

If **Option C** resonated most with you, then the Pioneer is probably your go to way of thinking. Its statements were:

- Is this even the right approach? There's got to be a smarter way.
- This brief is too narrow; we're solving the wrong problem.
- I challenge the thinking because possibility always feels worth chasing.

This Autopilot doesn't rush in or freeze up; it challenges the whole frame. When it takes the wheel and things get messy, you don't just look for solutions; you look for better questions.

From the Pioneer's perspective, the real danger isn't making the wrong move; it's solving the wrong problem.

Psychologists have found that when people feel stuck or limited, the brain often leaps to novelty, not out of boredom, but to regain a sense of agency and to feel in control.

The Pioneer loop kicks in when the current path feels too narrow. It scans for fresh angles, smarter alternatives and new ways through.

Imagine you're in a meeting.

The group's converging and the path is almost locked in. And something in you says: 'Hang on. What if we're solving the wrong thing?' For the Pioneer, moving forward is important, but only if it feels meaningful. Progress isn't the goal, purpose is. Otherwise, what's the point?

When it works, The Pioneer is the spark. It reframes the stuck situation and challenges sluggish thinking. It also sees possibilities no one else thought to look for.

You might recognise the pattern if you've thought:

- What if we're asking the wrong question?
- Let's step back. There's a better way to frame this.
- I've got one more idea; just hear me out.

If you're defaulting to this Autopilot, you're not trying to disrupt. You're trying to make it better.

What your brain is protecting is purpose (solving what actually matters), progress (but only if it's smarter) and creative momentum (because being stuck feels like going backwards).

When this Autopilot takes over, you keep scanning for the better path because committing too soon feels like closing the door on something great. But sometimes, the win was already on the table. And, the search for 'better' or 'different' quietly becomes a way to avoid choosing at all.

The following situation may sound familiar.

You're halfway through booking a trip and suddenly, you start rethinking the whole destination. You're in a meeting that's five minutes from the end and you pitch a whole new angle.

You don't do this because the current plan is broken, but because it doesn't feel inspired. That's your Pioneer at work.

This Autopilot is not trying to be difficult.

It's just trying to protect you from missing out on something awesome that hasn't yet been surfaced.

The Connector Autopilot: When coherence feels like safety

If **Option D** felt familiar, then the Connector may be a pattern you know well. Its statements were:

- We haven't even started, and I can already feel people pulling in different directions.

- If we don't align first, I'll have to hold everything together.

- I sense the drift early because holding the group together is what keeps us moving.

This Autopilot doesn't leap into action or chase data; it widens the lens. If this is your go-to thinking pattern, when things start to fragment, your instinct isn't to push forward. It's to hold things steady. To reconnect the people, the logic and the meaning, before it all starts to slip.

Psychologists and neuroscientists have found that when the world feels chaotic, humans instinctively seek shared meaning. It's not always about facts or outcomes; it's about whether everything fits together.

The Connector thinking pattern lives there. It doesn't care about control and instead, wants to keep the system whole.

The chances are that you've experienced the following more than once.

The conversation starts drifting. People talk at each other, and you can tell they're not on the same page. The purpose starts to wobble and your brain fires: *'Hang on, we're losing the thread.'*

For the Connector, the risk isn't delay or confusion; it's fragmentation. Losing the logic. Losing the people. Losing the plot.

When it works, the Connector Autopilot is the glue. It builds bridges, reframes meaning and keeps people, ideas and direction aligned —especially when things are ambiguous or complex.

You might recognise this way of thinking if you've thought:

- This doesn't feel joined up yet.
- Let me just re-explain so we're on the same page.
- If we move now, someone's going to fall out.

When this Autopilot is in full swing, you're not resisting the decision. You're trying to protect what holds it together.

What your brain is protecting includes coherence and meaning, relational and intellectual alignment, and connection to people, ideas and the bigger picture.

However, when this Autopilot takes over, you keep weaving the threads because letting go feels like letting the whole thing fray. But sometimes, the need to hold it all together can stop it from moving at all.

Perhaps this has happened to you.

You've paused a family decision with, 'Wait… is this really what we all want?' Or circled back in a meeting to reframe the logic because you could feel people drifting.

That's your Connector at work. Not trying to control, just trying to protect coherence when things start to come apart.

And let's face it. That is exhausting!

The Optimiser Autopilot: When precision feels like safety

If you were drawn towards **Option E**, then the Optimiser is likely to be one of your defaults. Its statements were:

- This is already messy; if we don't clean it up, we'll screw it up.

- If we rush this, we'll regret it later.

- I tighten things quickly because if it's not sharp, it won't hold.

This Autopilot doesn't leap ahead or zoom out; it sharpens. When things feel uncertain, your brain doesn't look for speed, it looks for precision.

Why?

Because if it's not completely right, it's not safe.

Research shows that when the pressure's on, some brains try to manage risk by tightening the details. The Optimiser pattern focuses in, not to stall, but to protect the outcome. It slows the momentum just long enough to make sure it holds.

The work may be close and a decision nearly there. But your brain fires: *'It's not ready yet. Let me just fix this one thing.'*

For the Optimiser, the perceived danger isn't delay; it's landing something that doesn't hold under scrutiny.

Half-baked feels worse than not done at all.

When applied to the right situation, the Optimiser raises the standard. It spots the flaw before it breaks, polishes the story and protects the result.

You might recognise this kind of thinking if you've thought:

- It's not quite there yet; just one more tweak.
- Let me tighten this; it needs to land clean.
- We can't send this yet; it has to be perfect.

When this is your default pattern, you're not obsessing over details. You're trying to protect quality under pressure.

What your brain is really protecting is progress (but only if it's clean), productivity (defined as quality, not speed) and control over how the work lands.

When this Autopilot takes over, you keep refining, not because it significantly changes the outcome, but because calling it done feels unsafe.

However, sometimes the real win isn't in the next tweak. It's in letting it go.

Have you ever rewritten a birthday message three times because 'it's not quite right yet.' Or delayed sending a proposal because 'one more edit might land it better'…even as the deadline ticks past.

That's your Optimiser at work. Not trying to hold things up. It's just trying to protect you by making sure things land 'just right'.

FROM HELPFUL TO HIJACKED

When it comes to The Answer Trap, the ability to recognise your default Autopilot is critical. If you can't see it, you can't interrupt it.

When the pressure's on, your brain will quietly drift into the thinking pattern it's comfortable with, even if it's no longer what the situation needs.

And, as we touched on earlier, this hijacks the way you see the situation. How you perceive what is going on, your interpretation of what it means and the kind of answers you look for.

Autopilot	What feels safe	What it does	What it cares about	Risk when in charge
Driver	Momentum	Push forward	Progress and control	Moving too fast, missing the point
Fact-Finder	Certainty	Pause and check	Accuracy and risk reduction	Can't know everything; delay without clarity
Pioneer	Possibility	Reframe the problem	Solving what matters	Avoiding decisions, chasing better forever
Connector	Coherence	Hold things together	Shared meaning and alignment	Slowing down too much to keep things intact
Optimiser	Precision	Sharpen the quality	Quality and how it lands	Never done enough, stuck in refinement

At some point in this chapter, you may have thought to yourself, *'Hang on, I use all five thinking patterns depending on the situation.'*

You're absolutely right. We all do.

The point is that one or two often come more naturally to us. So, when your brain feels under threat, it defaults to them. It's a fast, protective response.

Your Autopilot feels like the smart part of you, the one that knows how to navigate the situation you're in. This is what makes it so hard to spot when it's actually getting in the way.

In the next chapter, we'll look at what that moment feels like from the inside: how your Autopilot pulls *you* into the trap and what it takes to catch it before it takes you to the wrong place.

MAKE IT REAL

Take a moment to reflect on your top two Autopilot thinking patterns.
How familiar do they feel to you?

_____

_____

_____

Can you think of any examples where one or both Autopilots have dominated your thinking, without you realising it?

_____

_____

_____

How do those Autopilots impact your behaviour when faced with an ambiguous or complex situation under pressure?

_____

_____

_____

Key takeaway:

Each Autopilot is trying to help. But when it quickly and quietly takes over, it narrows your thinking. You stop responding to what's really happening and start reaching for relief instead of genuine clarity. *That's how you slide into The Answer Trap.*

CHAPTER IN A NUTSHELL

- When things get messy, your brain doesn't wait for instructions; it defaults to a protective pattern called your Cognitive Autopilot.

- These Autopilots are fast thinking loops designed to keep you safe, not necessarily to help you think clearly.

- There are five core patterns: the Driver, the Fact-Finder, the Pioneer, the Connector and the Optimiser, each triggered by a different belief about what matters most in the moment.

- Your Autopilot isn't a flaw. However, when it takes over, it narrows your thinking and steers you toward relief, not clarity.

- That's when The Answer Trap begins: when you stop responding to what the moment needs and start reacting from habit.

CHAPTER 10
THE DRIFT INTO DEFAULT

The headline landed at 6.47am: *'CEO accused of bullying and intimidation, says anonymous former exec.'*

By 7.15, three journalists had contacted the media line. The Chair called an emergency Board meeting for 8.45am.

It's now 8.41. One by one, the directors are arriving. Some are already in the room, others still walking in.

None of them are thinking clearly. And yet, each believes they are.

They've all read the headline. But what they're really responding to isn't the facts. It's the internal feeling of threat. To the company. To their role. To their ability to get from A to B. That instinctive quest for more of what they want and less of what they don't.

This particular morning, the latter is in focus.

The Answer Trap doesn't begin with shouting. It begins with the confidence of *perceived* clarity.

AUTOPILOTS IN ACTION

The people you're about to meet aren't personality types. They're directors, each pulled by a different cognitive pattern when the pressure rises. What you're seeing isn't who they are, but how their Autopilot narrows their view when uncertainty takes hold. And none of them know it's happening.

Director 1: The Driver

> He's early…but not by much. Just enough to walk in steady and look like he's already got a handle on things. Everyone's going to be looking for direction, including the Chair. She needs him.

> He's already half written the response in his head: 'Suspend pending review. Independent inquiry. Media holding line ready to go.'

> It's not about being first. It's about not looking lost.

> He knows how this goes. Wait too long and someone else controls the story. If you leave a vacuum, it gets filled.

> Everyone else will want to talk. Reflect. The usual people will get stuck in the weeds and others will want to talk about values. But, in his mind, that's not what the company needs right now. It needs to look like someone's in charge.

He's not trying to dominate. He's just trying to stop the drift before anyone opens their mouth.

Director 2: The Fact-Finder

She's been in the room for fifteen minutes. She's already read the background pack twice. And... she doesn't like what's missing.

The details are thin, and the risks aren't spelled out. The Chair's briefing was short. Too short. Someone's going to push to act quickly. They always do.

She can feel the unease rising because she knows how it goes when people move without seeing the full picture. Her job isn't to slow things down. It's to stop them from stepping into something blindly.

She doesn't need all the answers. She just needs a bit more clarity before they do something they can't undo.

Director 3: The Pioneer

He's walking in with the paper folded under his arm. He hasn't read it yet, not because he doesn't care, but because he already knows what it says. Same story, different day. Blah, blah, blah! They will focus on the surface and react quickly, entirely missing the bigger picture.

He's already asking the question no one else will: 'Is this really about one incident, or is this the symptom of something we haven't wanted to see?'

The others will play it safe. Protecting reputations. Trying to contain it. He's not here to manage the optics. He's here to challenge the lens through which everyone is looking. They'll probably think he's going off track. Again.

Someone needs to ask the uncomfortable questions. If they don't now, they'll regret it later.

Director 4: The Connector

He's already listening. Not just to what people say, but to what they mean.

Joe will push. He always does, wanting to keep everything moving. Maya will question everything. But that's because uncertainty makes Maya feel useful. And Sarah? The Chair. Sarah's holding her breath for just a second too long between sentences. That means she doesn't know where this is going either.

He's already starting to translate in his head what will be said when the meeting starts. 'So, what I'm hearing is that we need to move, but no one trusts the foundation we're standing on. And underneath all of this is one question: how do we act without breaking trust?'

He's not doing it for validation. He's doing it because if someone doesn't bring the pieces together, they'll each follow their own thread and the whole thing will unravel. He's already preparing to speak. Not to offer yet another opinion, but to connect what no one else has joined up yet.

Director 5: The Optimiser

She's got the draft comms on her screen and a tight feeling in her chest. It's not ready.

The language is completely off. The message is muddy. It's too reactive and somehow, not reactive enough. She knows they're going to want to move quickly, but if they send this out as is, it'll backfire. You only get one chance to land the first message.

She's not trying to hold things up. She just wants to make sure they don't make it worse. Because once this is out there, they won't get to explain. They'll just get judged. If that happens, she's not sure the company, or she, can stand behind it.

So now, everyone's in the room and the meeting is about to begin. But the trap?

That was triggered long before anyone sat down.

THE MEETING

The minute Sarah declares the meeting open, the drift begins.

Joe, the Driver, leans forward.

> 'We need to move, clean and fast. I propose we suspend, announce an independent review and finalise a holding statement today. The longer we wait, the more ground we lose.'

David, the Optimiser, lifts his head.

> 'I get the urgency, but the comms we've seen aren't sharp enough. If we move too fast, we'll regret it. I'd rather send nothing than send something that makes it worse.'

Jules, the Connector, steps in.

> 'Maybe what we need is to pause, just for a second. I'm hearing different priorities already: momentum, message, trust. Can we align before we act?'

Mark, the Pioneer, exhales.

> 'We're dancing around the core issue. This isn't just about the message. It's about what it reveals. If we don't address the cultural signals here, the media will do it for us.'

Elena, the Fact-Finder, chimes in.

> 'I don't think we even have the facts straight. We've got an anonymous source and no internal clarity. We're guessing at shadows. That's dangerous.'

Joe cuts back in.

> 'Doing nothing is dangerous too. The media won't wait for us to feel ready.'

There's a pause. Sarah, the Chair, listens. She asks clarifying questions. She reflects back what she hears. But something's already happening.

The group isn't choosing a direction. They're gravitating toward a compromise, one that includes a bit of everyone's opinion, but none of the real conversation.

They land on a statement.

It's cautious, technically sound and...deeply unmemorable. It buys time, avoids blame but says very little. They feel relieved. The meeting ends.

***

Let's pause here for a second.

Whether or not you've ever been in a Board meeting doesn't matter.

What played out here wasn't about titles or governance; it was about humans. This is what the brain does when we're faced with a high-stakes, ambiguous, complex moment. It moves rapidly, narrows in then grabs onto what feels safest.

So, take a breath and think about your own experience.

MAKE IT REAL:

Can you recall a time when you walked into a conversation, or a decision, already convinced you knew what was needed?

_____

_____

_____

How did that influence the way you engaged in the discussion?

_____

_____

_____

Have you ever sat in a group and felt like people were talking past each other? What Autopilots might have been running in the background, shaping each person's perspective and contribution?

_____

_____

_____

What role might your own Autopilots have played in your behaviour and experience?

_____

_____

_____

Key takeaway:

When the pressure hits, it's easy to confuse motion with clarity. But unless we notice our own defaults and name what's really happening in the room, we risk drifting into decisions that feel safe, but solve nothing.

What really happened in the Board meeting?

The Autopilots didn't appear when the meeting began. They emerged much earlier, when each member of the Board learned about the media story. From that point on, their thinking began to narrow. Not because they weren't competent, experienced directors; quite the opposite. Each of them had rich expertise and cared deeply. Yet, they each defaulted to the pattern that usually helped them feel in control.

Consequently, each director arrived with a quiet sense of what needed to happen next.

- The Driver needed to move.
- The Fact-Finder needed more clarity.
- The Pioneer needed to challenge the frame.
- The Connector needed to hold the system together.
- The Optimiser needed to get it right.

As far as each director was concerned, they weren't reacting; they were doing their job.

But no one asked themselves the most important question: What kind of thinking does this moment actually need from me?

So, as each of their Autopilots quietly took over, the directors' thinking became trapped. This meant that by the time Sarah opened the meeting, the outcome was already bending in five different directions.

The Board was at a fork in the road. Instead of thinking in a way that recognised it, the Autopilots led each mind down the most familiar path. The moment to choose differently was missed.

Eventually, the crisis with the CEO faded out of the media. But the culture of bullying and harassment continued. Until the next crisis and then… it all happened again.

WHY WE STOP THINKING

We live in a world of accelerating, cumulative disruption and our brain wasn't built for it.

We expect it to just cope and keep functioning as everything speeds up and shifts beneath our feet. But it can't. At least, not without consequences.

Remember Chapter 8? The one with the coffee shop example where, we explored how your brain moves between five different thinking modes to navigate daily life. These modes help you get from Point A to Point B, achieving more of what you want and less of what you don't.

In stable environments, your brain draws on:

- Doing mode when it's time to act
- Solving mode when something needs to be fixed
- Learning mode when something feels unfamiliar
- Exploring mode when you're scanning for new ideas
- Sensemaking mode when things feel off and you need to understand why

This kind of cognitive flexibility is what allows you to adapt, respond and move forward with clarity in real time.

But that's not what happens under pressure.

*When disruption piles up, your brain begins to lose
the very thing you most need in complex scenarios:
flexibility.*

Instead of shifting between different modes of thinking based on what the situation requires, it narrows and locks in. It does what it's always done to protect you. Trigger the thinking it trusts the most.

So how does this pull you into The Answer Trap? And, what role does your Autopilot play?

How you fly in

We've already established that The Answer Trap is a cognitive state where your brain stops thinking when thinking is most needed. It doesn't stop because you've reached genuine clarity. It stops because you've found something – an answer, an action or a direction – that feels clear enough to ease the discomfort.

When your brain is under pressure, without a way to think flexibly, it hands control to your Autopilot. It's your brain's shortcut – an instinctive pattern that's been useful before. But in disruption, that shortcut flies you straight into The Answer Trap.

Here's how it happens:

- *Complacency*

    Your Autopilot has worked, in less disrupted situations, many times before. That makes it feel safe, familiar and effective. So, your brain doesn't question whether it's still the best approach. It just assumes that it is.

- *Selectivity*

    Your Autopilot doesn't just narrow how you think – it narrows what you think you're looking for. It redefines what a 'good' answer means, based on what your brain is trying to protect. And once you find something that matches that definition, even if it's not the right fit, you feel relief. So, you stop looking.

- *Rigidity*

    You don't just look for a narrow kind of answer. You keep using a narrow kind of thinking. Your brain clings to one or two familiar modes, instead of switching to the mode the situation actually needs. That means even when you act, you're more likely to miss what matters.

- *Invisibility*

    Your Autopilot doesn't announce itself. It runs quietly in the background, like it's part of your normal thinking. So, you don't notice the moment your thinking shifts from flexible to fixed. You feel like you're being thoughtful when in fact, your brain has already stopped exploring.

That's exactly what happened in the Board scenario.

Each director walked in with their Autopilot already running. Unlike the coffee shop example, they weren't shifting flexibly between the five thinking modes. They had already locked in – and were unconsciously rejecting the rest.

- The Driver leaned hard into Doing, pushing for action and control.

- The Fact-Finder stayed in Learning, scanning for gaps and risks.

- The Pioneer stretched into Exploring, but resisted closure or compromise.

- The Optimiser zoomed in on precision, stuck between Doing and Solving.

- The Connector tried to fill gaps through Sensemaking but wasn't contributing anything new, just smoothing over what was there.

Each person was flying in a different mental direction. So, while it felt like a shared discussion, it was actually five separate conversations stitched loosely into one.

But unlike the Board members, you now have the edge.

You know how your Autopilot shows up and how easily it can hijack your thinking. Not by shutting it down, but by narrowing it so gradually you barely notice.

Once you can see it, you can start to interrupt it. And the opportunity?

It's not just avoiding poor decisions. It's reclaiming the clarity, energy and impact that become possible when you stop reacting from default patterns and start thinking deliberately.

But there's one uncomfortable truth.

The only person who can switch off your Autopilot… is you.

Which, of course, leads to the next question: How do you actually do that?

Here's where we go next

Part 3 is all about making the shift from *default* to *deliberate* thinking. It introduces a practical, proven approach to do what most people find incredibly difficult. That is, to break free from The Answer Trap and engage the kind of thinking that complex, ambiguous situations demand.

Not once or every now and then. But consistently, both on your own, and with others.

So, let's keep going.

CHAPTER IN A NUTSHELL

- The Answer Trap doesn't usually start with chaos; it often starts with a premature sense of certainty driven by our Autopilot.

- Under pressure, your brain narrows its focus to a familiar thinking mode that feels safe, even if it's not what the situation requires.

- These default responses, your Autopilot patterns, aren't wrong in themselves, but they become rigid under pressure and resist other necessary ways of thinking.

- In groups, this leads to mismatched thinking. Everyone's contributing, but often no one's participating in the same underlying conversation.

- The result? Misalignment, muddled decisions, wasted energy and a false sense of clarity or progress.

- Breaking free starts by noticing when your thinking has defaulted, because if you can't see it, you can't consciously shift it.

PART 3:

MASTER YOUR MOMENT

THE CRITICAL QUESTION

ACTIVATE

ARTICULATE

NAVIGATE

PART 3: WHAT TO EXPECT

We've spent the first sections of our journey exploring the often-invisible current that pulls us off course – The Answer Trap. We've seen how it works, why it feels so compelling (even when it leads us astray) and how easily we can fall into its grip, especially when pressure and complexity rise. We've even lifted the lid on our brain to understand a bit more about our own mental wiring and the Autopilot thinking patterns that kick in automatically.

Recognising the trap is a huge first step. But as we discussed, awareness alone, while crucial, often isn't enough to break free when you're caught in the turbulence of a messy moment.

Knowing you're sliding doesn't automatically give you the footing to stop.

That's what this Part is all about. We're shifting from diagnosis to action. From understanding the problem to learning a practical, repeatable way to navigate *through* it. This is where we roll up our sleeves and dive into the core toolkit designed for exactly these situations: The Moment Method.

Over the next few chapters, we'll focus on building the foundational skills you need to master your *own* thinking in real-time. We'll unpack the first three crucial levels – Activate, Articulate and Navigate.

These are the moves that allow you to interrupt your Autopilot, define what truly matters in the midst of confusion and consciously guide your brain toward clarity, even when the path isn't obvious.

Learning to manage your own internal state and thinking process under pressure is the bedrock. It's the foundation upon which everything else, including influencing group dynamics (covered later), is built. Most importantly, it's how you start to take back control, not necessarily of the external situation, but of your own response to it.

Ready to get practical?

To gain the most value from Part 3, I suggest that you take advantage of the *Make it real* sections and don't rush. The goal is to build your capability piece by piece, even week by week.

It's better to take one idea and apply it, than it is to plough ahead, feel overwhelmed and then, change nothing.

So, let's start by understanding the method itself.

CHAPTER 11
THE MOMENT METHOD

Have you ever noticed how musicals tend to divide people?

You either love them or you don't. I'm in the former camp, and one of my favourites is *Jekyll & Hyde*. There's a scene where the main character stands centre stage, music swelling, arms lifted to the heavens, singing:

'*This is the moment.*'

It's a great song. And it captures a popular idea: that a moment is something grand or cinematic. A turning point you usually recognise in hindsight, once you know what came after.

But the kind of moment we're talking about in this book is different.

The Moment is a point in time when disruption interferes with your ability to move from A to B. It's when the path you were following is no longer clear, possible, viable or optimal. And your brain feels it.

The Moment doesn't begin with drama.

It starts with a flicker. We've talked about it a few times. That internal signal that something has shifted. You might notice disorientation, tension or frustration. That is the beginning.

The Moment ends when you can answer the question: *What needs to happen now?*

That answer might involve restoring your original path. Or it might mean rebuilding a new one, or reimagining where you're going altogether. But until that point, you are in what I call The Fog of Uncertainty. Your brain is searching for something solid to hold onto. Without it, it will default to whatever feels fast, safe or familiar.

Most importantly, *The Moment* is that fleeting window of opportunity to do something different, that frankly, most of us miss.

This is the space The Moment Method is designed for.

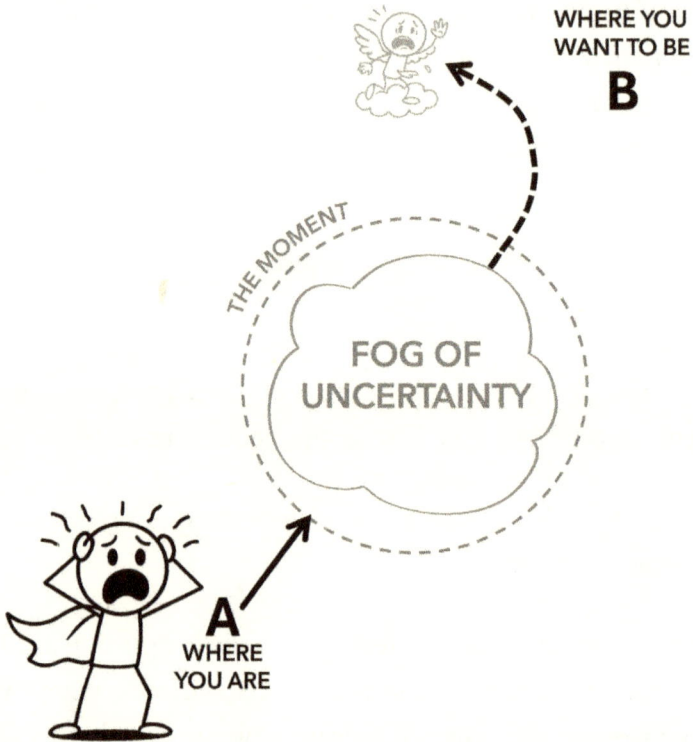

WHERE YOU WANT TO BE

B

THE MOMENT

FOG OF UNCERTAINTY

A
WHERE YOU ARE

TURBULENCE WITHOUT TRAINING

This need for real-time awareness isn't unique to business or leadership. It shows up in everyday life too. I was reminded of this a few years ago when I was leading a multi-day strategy event for a team based in Tucson, Arizona.

The team had been navigating heavy disruption, so to break things up, they spent an afternoon at the Pima Air & Space Museum. One of the team members had invited their daughter to join the trip. She was a young pilot-in-training, and she agreed to share a few insights with the group.

She talked about learning to fly in uncertain skies. Not just how to operate the plane, but how to think clearly when conditions change quickly.

Pilots, she explained, are trained to expect turbulence. They are taught to recognise what it feels like when instinct kicks in, and to catch themselves when they want to react too quickly. They are also taught to spot what the aviation industry calls 'hazardous attitudes.' These are common thought patterns like 'I've got this,' or 'It won't happen to me.'

Part of pilot training is learning how to notice these mental reflexes and choose something more useful instead.

At the time, I couldn't help but draw a parallel between the young pilot's words and the environment in which many of us find ourselves.

We're not flying planes, but our brains hit turbulence all the time. However, unlike pilots, most of us have never been trained to recognise the early warning signs.

The flicker. The red flags. The point where thinking starts to tighten and instinct begins to take over.

Instead, we feel it without understanding it. The disruption comes, but we don't see how it works. It feels sudden and seems to come out of nowhere. Just like turbulence.

Most passengers on a plane know what turbulence is, in a general sense. We understand that it's got something to do with air pressure and unstable currents. But for most people, turbulence still feels mysterious. You don't know when it will happen or how to respond. You just hold on and hope the plane steadies itself.

Pilots are different. They are taught what causes turbulence, how to see it coming and what to do when they fly into it.

The Moment Method does the same thing in the context of human disruption.

It helps you understand what's happening inside your mind, why it's happening and what to do next. Not only that, it also takes the mystery out of disruption itself, showing its unseen yet often predictable patterns. This unlocks the capacity to act intentionally, make choices and to influence outcomes, rather than simply being acted upon by the turbulence around you.

In this way, The Moment Method doesn't just give you awareness, it gives you agency by providing the ability to work with disruption in real time.

So, let's take a closer look at why it works.

THREE WAYS WE GET STUCK

You've already met your Autopilot and have seen how it narrows your view and blocks other ways of thinking. When we encounter The Moment, but we don't understand it, our brain does one of three things.

Unlike the Autopilots, these aren't patterns of preference. They're signs your brain is losing traction inside The Moment and your thinking starts to slip.

You might experience one or all of them.

- **Collapse**

  This is when you zoom in too far. Your brain locks onto a narrow part of the situation – something it feels it can manage. You might fixate on details, tasks or immediate actions, even if they are not what The Moment really calls for. Collapse helps you feel productive, but it often means you're avoiding what actually matters.

- **Drift**

  In this pattern, you lose the thread. You might feel scattered, foggy or confused. Your brain jumps from one task or concern to another, responding to noise rather than meaning. You are moving but not going anywhere useful.

- **Slide**

  Slide happens when the discomfort gets too loud. You start chasing relief rather than clarity. You latch onto the emotion (eg. frustration, urgency, fear) and then follow it, often without knowing you've done it. You react instead of responding. You end up off-track, asking 'How did I get here?', but can't pinpoint when or how it happened.

These reactions are protective. They're your brain's way of trying to find its way through the turbulence without any training.

But what do you need in that internal state, when your brain has started to collapse, drift or slide?

Not more insight. You often already have that. Not more willpower, because that runs out quickly when pressure builds.

You need something that works in real time and helps your brain shift from simply noticing the situation to actually working with it.

In short, you need three things:

- **Space**

  Room to interrupt the reflex and engage your thinking. Without space, your brain keeps speeding up or locking in. Space slows The Moment just enough for awareness to become useful.

- **Structure**

  A way to re-centre your focus. Structure gives your brain a reference point. It helps you know where you are, what matters, and what kind of thinking the situation needs. Without it, you stay scattered or stuck.

- **Strategies**

  Practical tools to help you keep thinking usefully through the mess. These are not magic answers. They are small, repeatable moves that help your brain stay constructive, even when the path ahead is unclear.

These three elements give your brain something to hold onto, work with and guide your thinking forward, instead of flapping around in the fog. They sit at the core of The Moment Method and unlock your capacity to act and make independent choices when you find yourself in unknown.

This is what makes the shift from awareness to agency possible.

MAKE IT REAL

So, think about the last time you found yourself facing The Moment when your existing path from A to B was no longer an option. Was there evidence of:

Collapse - zooming in too far? Drift - losing the thread? Slide - chasing relief?

_____

_____

What might have shifted if your brain had a Copilot beside it - one that knew how to steady the thinking, not just speed it up?

_____

_____

Key takeaway:

Collapse, Drift and Slide aren't failures… they're signals. The Moment Method helps you catch them early and shift from reactive to deliberate thinking, right when it matters most.

FROM AUTOPILOT TO COPILOT

There's an important point to be made here, because what we've talked about so far goes beyond better thinking techniques. It's a paradigm shift. One that involves changing the relationship you have with your thinking and developing a better working partnership with your brain.

In Autopilot, your brain takes over. It runs rapidly, follows familiar patterns and makes snap decisions on your behalf. And most of the time, we let it because it works. However, in high-pressure situations that are ambiguous and complex – it doesn't work.

In these messy situations, we need a different thinking paradigm. I call it 'Copilot'.

In Copilot, you don't fight your brain - you partner with it. Just like the young pilot learned, it's not about overriding instinct - it's about noticing it early and working with it consciously. You give it direction, not resistance and stay present long enough to think deliberately, instead of lapsing into default thinking.

It becomes a symbiotic relationship because in return, your brain gives you what you actually need: clarity, perspective and a path forward that's right for The Moment, not just the familiar pattern.

This isn't about outsmarting your instincts or pretending they aren't there or don't matter. It's about using and refocusing them, with intention.

And that shift - from Autopilot to Copilot - is exactly what The Moment Method helps you make.

A PRACTICAL APPROACH

The Moment Method didn't start as something I planned to teach or share. It started as a survival strategy - crystallised over 30 years of navigating disruption for a living.

Long before it had a name, I was building it in real time: as a leader, advisor and human inside high-stakes environments where clarity was hard to come by and guaranteed answers were a highly prized commodity.

The approach didn't come from a theory – that came later. It came from pressure, experience and moments where the cost of reactive thinking became all too clear.

From noticing exactly when things went off track - like the time I had a mutiny on one of my programs where all the technical experts refused to get involved - and recognising the rising panic and reactivity in my own mind.

In truth, much of The Moment Method came from the pain of falling into The Answer Trap myself and getting important decisions wrong. And, seeing those around me do exactly the same.

Over time, I started decoding these situations.

I paid attention to what worked, what helped me recover, what helped others stay clear. I also noticed how deliberate thinking, when done effectively, could shift the thinking of a room full of people in a matter of minutes.

That's how The Moment Method took shape. It's a real-time practice that helps your brain find its way through the unknown without defaulting to familiar patterns or forced answers.

It gives your brain those three elements that The Answer Trap takes away: Space, Structure and Strategy.

How it works

The Moment Method helps you find clarity when it matters most, stay steady when things get messy and choose your next move with intention, not just instinct.

By now, you've already encountered pieces of the approach throughout the book.

In Part 1 we explored the consequences of the human brain's ability to deal with messy moments and how that, accelerated by technology, is luring us into The Answer Trap.

That insight is foundational because as I've said before, if you can't see the trap and don't know how it happens, you can't do anything about it.

Then came the A to B framework. You saw how your brain constantly tries to close the gap between where you are and where you want to be. And what happens when disruption hits, throwing your thinking off course. You've met the five thinking modes and you've seen how they help you navigate the gap, and how pressure can block the very modes you most need.

You've also met your Autopilot and seen how it leans on one or two familiar thinking modes, while unconsciously rejecting the rest.

All of this builds toward one core capability: the ability to notice when your thinking is drifting, and to choose how you respond. That's what The Moment Method is for.

Just as the young pilot in Tucson learned to recognise and work with her instincts to navigate turbulence, we need to train our brains to operate effectively in today's unpredictable environment.

That's where *meta-cognition* comes in.

Meta-cognition simply means being able to observe and guide your own thinking. Not just *what* you think, but *how* you think in The Moment. Without that skill, falling into The Answer Trap becomes almost inevitable.

Having progressed this far in the book, you now have the language and awareness to begin working with your mind in a different way.

A key part of this shift is learning to see The Moment. Not just noticing it but actually visualising it.

When the world feels unclear or chaotic, your brain instinctively reverts to familiar patterns. To interrupt that reflex, your brain needs a new framework. That's where the Moment Model comes in.

---

*In unknown terrain, your brain doesn't just need a
new path. It needs a way to build a new map.*

The Moment Model helps you locate yourself in your own thinking and gives you a sense of where you are, what kind of thinking the situation calls for and what comes next. It's a way to move from the scramble for fast (and often flawed) answers, to a more grounded, useful structure for regaining clarity.

Of course, a framework is only helpful if it's something you can actually use. It's designed to help you not just understand the concept but apply it in real time. When disruption triggers The Moment, typically one of three things happens.

We either:

- *Miss it* – We don't realise the internal shift has happened until it's too late.
- *Muddle through* – We rely on instinct and hope it's enough.
- *Master it* – We direct our thinking consciously, even when things are tough.

The Moment Method enables you to master the moments that matter. But here, mastery doesn't mean being in control of the situation - it means staying clear-headed and intentional in how you think, regardless of what's happening around you.

The Moment Method gives you a structured way to make that shift.

It's how you move from being swept along by the rip current to actively steering your thinking out of it.

In the next few chapters, we'll talk about the three foundational levels that help you build this skill:

- **Activate**

  Creates space in the mind. It interrupts your usual reactions and helps you reorient. The signal: 'This doesn't feel familiar - I need to think differently.'

- **Articulate**

  Helps you shape a meaningful starting point by clarifying what matters most and naming the core tension. It's the cognitive foothold that gets you moving in the right direction.

- **Navigate**

  Keeps you thinking clearly and constructively while things remain uncertain. It supports progress without rushing to closure or forcing certainty too soon.

These levels aren't about perfect thinking. They're about staying engaged, managing your inner state and making deliberate choices when it counts. And, when repeated often, these steps evolve into a repeatable practice you can call on whenever complexity gets in your way.

Later in the book, we'll also explore how to apply these ideas to group dynamics, unlocking collaboration in high-stakes, ambiguous situations. But for now, the focus is on building a solid personal foundation.

With that in place, let's step into the first level of the method – **Activate** – and learn how to recognise The Moment when your thinking needs to shift.

CHAPTER IN A NUTSHELL

- The Moment isn't a dramatic event. It's a window of opportunity where disruption affects your ability to move from A to B, and you choose to lead your thinking instead of defaulting to habit.

- It begins with a flicker, an internal cue that something has changed, and ends when you can answer, 'What needs to happen now?'

- When you miss The Moment, your brain often falls into Collapse, Drift or Slide. These are protective patterns, but they can trap you in false clarity.

- What your brain needs in that space is not more insight or willpower. It needs space, structure and strategies to support deliberate thinking.

- The Moment Method helps you shift from Autopilot to Copilot. It gives you the tools to stay present, partner with your brain and engage usefully in the moment.

- Metacognition is the key. By learning to observe and guide your thinking, you build the mental map needed to navigate uncertainty.

- You can miss the moment, muddle through it or master it. The Moment Method helps you do the latter, not through control, but through clarity.

- The next chapters walk you through the three core levels: Activate, Articulate and Navigate. Each one is designed to build your capacity for real-time thinking in disruption.

CHAPTER 12
ACTIVATE

Remember the story of Barry Marshall?

The doctor who ultimately proved that stomach ulcers were caused by bacteria, not just stress, challenging decades of medical belief?

Long before Dr Marshall famously drank the bacteria culture, he did something quieter but arguably more important: he *caught The Moment*. He recognised the nagging possibility that everything he and the entire medical community had been taught about ulcers might be incomplete, or even wrong. And crucially, he allowed that uncomfortable possibility to challenge his thinking, rather than dismissing it.

In that initial moment of doubt, Marshall didn't have a five-step plan. He didn't know for sure that bacteria was the answer, or what the path forward would look like. He just had an inkling, a feeling that something didn't quite add up.

That's often how these moments begin. Not with a flash of insight or a clear solution, but with a small internal shift you can barely put your finger on.

Dr Marshall didn't miss it, but he easily could have. Imagine him sitting in a conference, surrounded by esteemed colleagues. He could have just nodded along, reinforcing the accepted wisdom, 'Yes, of course. Ulcers are caused by stress and lifestyle. We know this.' That would have been the easier path, the one of least resistance.

It's The Answer Trap,
presenting itself as established fact.

That pull towards the familiar, the accepted, is exactly why Activation is the critical first step in breaking free.

This chapter will get you started. More specifically, it will show you how to catch The Moment, before it catches you.

ACTIVATION: CREATING THE SPACE TO CHOOSE

So, what exactly *is* Activation in the context of The Moment Method?

It's the deliberate act of scanning for, then noticing when one of these internal shifts (a potential 'moment') has begun, *before* your thinking automatically slides into its default patterns.

It starts with catching that first flicker of discomfort, uncertainty or reaction. You don't need to understand The Moment fully at this stage; you just need to recognise that *something* internally has shifted.

The core purpose of Activation is deceptively simple but incredibly powerful. It's about consciously creating space. The space to:

- notice the trigger (a disruption happening) and your habitual response.
- interrupt the Autopilot reflex and to breathe.
- move from simply reacting to consciously *choosing* how you want to engage your thinking next.

Activation works because *The Moment*, as we're exploring it, is often triggered by your own awareness. Asking yourself, internally, *'Hang on, could this be a moment?'* acts like pressing pause on your brain's Autopilot. It interrupts the reactive flow and shifts you into a more conscious, observant state.

You're no longer just being carried along by the current of your thoughts and feelings; you're choosing to notice the current itself.

That simple act changes your relationship with what's happening, opening the door to a different response.

WHY ACTIVATE?

Why is creating this initial space so critical? When faced with uncertainty or perceived threat (which is how the brain often interprets messy, ambiguous moments), the primary drive isn't sophisticated problem solving; it's achieving safety and reducing discomfort, fast.

This triggers immediate reactions:

- Your body might tense up.
- Your thoughts might race towards quick fixes or shut down.
- You feel an urge to *do something*, anything, to regain control.

Activation pushes back against this urge. It creates breathing room:

- When your heart starts racing with urgency, Activation gently says, *'Slow down for a second.'*
- When your brain screams, *'Find an answer, now!'*, Activation quietly insists, *'Not just yet.'*
- When your instincts yell, 'Do something, anything!', Activation counsels, 'Hold on. Let's see first.'

One of the subtle beauties of this approach is that when you intentionally Activate a moment, you give yourself explicit permission *not to know* immediately.

You're releasing the pressure to have the perfect response, immediately and on demand.

In doing so, you signal to your brain that it can stop grasping for the nearest certainty or the fastest way out. You're saying, 'This isn't about reacting, this is about thinking.'

These Moments rarely arrive with clarity. Instead, they often appear shrouded in that Fog of Uncertainty I mentioned earlier.

It's a bit like driving down the freeway at 110 kilometres an hour, with cruise control on - until you hit thick fog. You don't keep driving the same way. You switch off cruise control, slow down and adjust how you're navigating.

That's exactly what Activation does. It tells your brain: this is not business as usual. It's time to shift gears. And in doing so, it gives you the first essential ingredient for clear thinking: **space**.

NOT EVERY MOMENT NEEDS THE FULL TREATMENT

Now, does this mean you have to stop and meticulously Activate every single time you feel a flicker of uncertainty or discomfort throughout your day?

Absolutely not. That would be exhausting and impractical.

The Moment arises when disruption is present, whether or not you've consciously recognised it yet.

We all experience countless micro-moments of internal disruption ie. shifts in feeling or thought that come and go.

Remember the parent who was getting the kids ready for school a few chapters ago? And we talked about the four types of disruption?

1. **Activity disruption** – The *how* changes.

   The task and goal are still clear, but the method needs to shift.

2. **Task disruption** – The *what* changes.

   The job stays the same, but the task must change.

3. **Pattern disruption** – The routine breaks down.

   The job and tasks are still known, but nothing works as expected.

4. **Cumulative disruption** – The system breaks down.

   Disruption stacks up. The goal, the situation, and the path are unclear. Your usual thinking modes can't land because the frame keeps shifting.

Some of these disruptions genuinely throw us off balance. They demand attention. Others are just background noise, minor friction points your brain can navigate easily without intervention.

Using The Moment Method, starting with Activation, doesn't mean dissecting every small disruption. Instead, think of Activation as a 'pause button'. A way to notice those internal shifts more consistently, and to choose deliberately how to respond.

Here's the key.

The greater the breadth and depth of disruption (ie. it's more like Type 4 and less like Type 1), the more you need deliberate thinking. And yet, paradoxically, the less your brain is able to cope on its own. That's the tipping point.

Your default responses become unreliable just when you have the least clarity. That's why The Moment Method exists. Not for the easy moments, but for the ones your brain wasn't designed to handle alone.

You get to ask yourself:

- 'Okay, I feel that familiar tightening, rush or blankness. Is this signalling something that truly matters right now?'

- 'What type of disruption am I dealing with? What does that mean?'

- 'Is this a moment where reacting on default might lead me astray? Or is this something minor that I can handle adequately on Autopilot?'

Sometimes, the answer will be, 'Yes, this matters. I need to engage deliberately.' Other times, it might be, 'This is just friction. I can let this one go.'

The power lies in making that call consciously. Not just being swept along by habit. Activation gives you that discernment, and The Moment Method gives you the structure to back it up.

THE POWER OF CATCHING IT – EVEN LATE

Here's something liberating about Activation: you don't always have to catch The Moment perfectly at its very inception. Sometimes the internal reaction happens so quickly, or we're so distracted, that we only realise we're caught in a reactive pattern when we're already halfway down the path.

Maybe you're mid-argument and suddenly hear yourself saying something defensive you'll later regret. Maybe you're deep into executing a task and realise with a jolt that it feels pointless or misdirected. Maybe you've been feeling vaguely 'off' about a situation for days, pushing the feeling down, until it finally bubbles up undeniably.

Even then, you can still Activate and hit the pause button.

You're rarely truly 'too late'. Why?

The Moment isn't just a fixed point in external time; it's fundamentally about where you are now and your relationship to the current situation.

Imagine that you have a new boss who you don't get along with. You've been unhappy since they arrived, but that was months ago. It could be argued that The Moment started when you had the first meeting with your boss, and you walked away realising that you were both on different wavelengths.

At the time, you didn't do anything. Now, you're commuting home from work and think to yourself 'Ugh! I hate my job'.

The *second* you bring conscious attention to that thought on the train, of being off-kilter, reactive or stuck, the opportunity to Activate becomes available again. It's always about The Moment you're in now and the context within which it is happening, not a past moment that you could have responded to earlier.

This is a new moment. So, you can still say to yourself: *'Hang on. Something's not right here. Let me reset. Could this be a moment that I need to Activate?'*

You interrupt the pattern *where you are.* You create space *now* and choose to engage deliberately *from this point forward.* It's never too late to stop the slide and regain your footing.

THE FOUR ESSENTIAL MOVES

So, how do you *Activate*, especially when you feel that internal pressure mounting or realise you're already reacting?

It isn't just a vague intention to 'be more present'; it's a deliberate sequence. Think of it as four distinct moves that work together to interrupt the reactive slide and create that crucial space for clearer, more deliberate thinking.

They are: *Feel it, Name it, Calm it, Claim it.*

These four moves give you a way to interrupt the reactive pull when your brain reacts to disruption. But before we explore them in detail, it helps to understand what The Moment actually is, not just how it feels, but how it works.

The anatomy of The Moment

One of the first things I teach clients is what The Moment would look like under a microscope. That shift turns something abstract into something more tangible. It moves from being a vague feeling to something you can observe, name and work with.

Think of a cell that a scientist might examine. It has identifiable components, a shape and a consistent internal structure. Once you know what to look for, it becomes easier to spot and understand, even when the environment around it is complex.

Over the years, I've learnt that The Moment has its own anatomy. Even when the situation itself is unpredictable, The Moment tends to follow a recognisable pattern. Once you learn to see it, some of the fear and urgency start to fall away. You no longer feel completely adrift. Instead, you have a frame of reference.

That familiarity does not remove the discomfort, but it does make the terrain feel less threatening. It helps you shift from overwhelm to what I call *comfortable discomfort*. This is the mental space where you can tolerate uncertainty without needing to eliminate it, then stay engaged long enough to think clearly.

Most importantly, when The Moment has a visible structure, you can draw it.

Anything that gets The Moment out of your head
and into the world, where you can stand back from it,
becomes an essential thinking tool.

Recognising the structure of The Moment gives you something to work with. But how you choose to relate to it, especially when stepping into The Fog of Uncertainty, is just as important.

Before we break down the four moves in detail, let's take a look at the mindset that helps you apply them in real life.

Think like a surfer

I spent every childhood summer at a beach called Lilli Pilli on the south coast of New South Wales. After a morning in the water, I'd often wander the rocks and watch the surfers from the headland. I didn't realise it at the time, but the contrast between the swimmers and the surfers told a much bigger story than just who was in the water.

Swimmers and surfers both spend time in the water, but they relate to it in completely different ways.

A swimmer thrives in a pool. The lanes are marked, the water is still, and the goal is clear: move efficiently from one end to the other in a straight line. Progress is measured by rhythm, speed and control. There's very little uncertainty involved.

At worst, someone slower might drift into the fast lane, but even then, the disruption is minimal and doesn't really change how the swimmer approaches what they're doing or why they're there.

At Lilli Pilli, you'd sometimes see swimmers doing laps across the bay, but only when the water was flat. As soon as the swell picked up or the current shifted, they were back on the beach, lying on their towels and working on their tan instead.

Surfers, on the other hand, are drawn to the swell because calm water holds no appeal. They don't just *expect* turbulence, unpredictability and change – they crave it. Surfers study the ocean, watch the patterns, wait for the right moment and then move with purpose. When they fall, which they often do, they don't take it as failure. It's all part of the experience and so they climb back on, adjust, learn and adapt in real time.

That's the mindset Activation is built on. It's not about staying in control or having all the answers. You don't need to master every Moment or perform every move perfectly. You just need to stay in it long enough to find your balance and respond with intent.

So, now we've got the right mindset, let's come back to those four moves so you can go from *resisting* the wave to *riding* it.

Feel it: Tune in to your body's signal

Almost every messy moment registers *physically* before it registers as a fully formed thought. It starts with a feeling, often subtle. You've likely felt these signals I mentioned a few minutes ago, even if you didn't consciously label them:

- That slight tightening in your chest or a knot forming in your stomach.
- Your breathing becoming shallower, maybe faster.

- A sudden surge of urgency pushing you to act, even without clear direction.

- Or perhaps the opposite – a sudden mental blankness, a feeling of stalling.

This physical sensation isn't random noise. It's your body's early warning, signalling that your nervous system is reacting. Your first, critical move in Activation is simply to *notice* this feeling clearly and quickly, without judgment.

Don't rush past it. Don't try to ignore it or push it down. Just acknowledge its presence:

- 'There it is. I feel that tension/rush/blankness – something's shifted internally.'

You can't consciously engage with The Moment if you don't even realise your system is already responding. Recognising the physical signal is the entry point.

Name it: Step back by externalising the state

The second move helps pull you out of being *submerged* in the feeling and back into a position of observation. You give the internal state a simple label, clearly and explicitly. You can say it out loud if you're alone, or just state it firmly in your mind:

'Okay, this is a messy moment kicking in.'
'Right, I'm feeling that urge to react quickly.'
'This is my Autopilot starting to spin.'
'I'm noticing [stress/urgency/confusion] arising.'

Naming the state does something neurologically powerful – it   begins to externalise it. Why? Because when you can get the thinking out of your head and turn it into something you can stand back from, it helps you disconnect.

Instead of *being* overwhelmed, you are *observing* the feeling of over-whelm arise. You shift identity slightly, from 'I *am* stressed' to 'I am *noticing* stress.' That simple, deliberate act of labelling creates a sliver of mental distance, putting you back in the observer's seat, which is the first step towards regaining agency.

Calm it: Downshift your nervous system to enable thinking

This next move might feel counterintuitive, almost passive, especially when pressure is high, but it's arguably the most crucial for regaining cognitive function. Before you jump into doing or solving, you need to intentionally calm your physiological state.

Your brain simply cannot access its higher-level thinking capacities – strategic insight, creativity, nuanced judgement – if it's flooded with stress hormones and operating in survival mode (fight, flight or freeze).

I find the following approaches useful, but I recommend experimenting to find an approach that works for you.

- Take one slow, deliberate breath – imagining you're breathing in a circle, when the inward breath takes you to the top of the circle and the outward breath takes you to the bottom of it.
- Consciously ground your feet on the floor, feeling their solid connection.

- Briefly tense and release your shoulders or hands.

- Simply pause for 5-10 seconds, doing nothing but noticing your breath.

This isn't about achieving instant Zen. It's about sending a quick signal to your nervous system: *'We're not facing immediate physical danger right now.'*

This helps reduce the stress response just enough for your thinking brain (the Prefrontal Cortex) to start coming back online.

When I'm working with clients, they sometimes say that this sounds easier on paper than it is in reality. This is a natural response. However, when you understand the Moment Method and practice it, this move becomes easier. Why?

When you know that it's just 'a moment' and you know what a moment feels like, it becomes less unknown and feels less of a threat.

It gives a sense of confidence that you have a way to move forward. You're not going to get stuck, the threat feels lower and the instinctive reaction becomes less overwhelming.

In fact, as I share more about the Moment Method, you'll discover that it offers a way to turn that feeling of anxiety into anticipation, or even excitement. But that's something for later.

Claim it: Choose curiosity over escaping discomfort

Now comes the pivotal mental shift, the one that truly changes your relationship with disruption and its consequences.

You deliberately claim The Moment as something to engage with, rather than something to resist or escape from.

Instead of letting your default internal narrative be:

- 'Oh no, this feels bad/uncomfortable/uncertain. How do I get out of this feeling quickly?'

You consciously shift your stance towards curiosity and exploration:

- 'Okay, this feels messy/uncomfortable/uncertain. Instead of trying to immediately escape this feeling, what if I stay with it just a bit longer?
- What might I notice or learn if I choose curiosity right now?'

Claiming The Moment changes how your brain sees it. Just as a surfer engages with a wave, The Moment is no longer a threat to neutralise, but a challenge with the potential for discovery.

It signals something different:

- 'This isn't just something to escape. It's something I need to understand. Let's step in, not run away.'

You move from instinctively avoiding discomfort to consciously engaging with uncertainty. You begin to *own* it and instead of just being 'a' moment, it becomes 'your' moment.

It's the first critical step towards catching The Moment, instead of The Moment catching you.

Okay! So, now we've got our four Activation moves. Let's finish the chapter by discovering what they look like in practice.

FEEL IT	NAME IT	CALM IT	CLAIM IT
Tune in to your body's signal	Step back by externalising the state	Get your nervous system to stand down to enable thinking	Choose curiosity over escaping discomfort

ACTIVATION: AN EVERYDAY EXAMPLE

Imagine you're wrapping up your workday, ticking off those final items before heading out. It's been a demanding day, but there's a quiet sense of progress. You've kept the essential plates spinning, cleared what needed clearing, and carved out just enough mental space to begin letting go.

Tonight matters. It's your partner's birthday dinner. You promised yourself you'd be present. Not just in the room, but really there. No distracted scrolling. No work talk over entrees. Just a full shift into your evening life.

Then your phone buzzes.

It's a message from your boss: 'Need to talk first thing tomorrow 8am sharp. Cancel other plans. Urgent.'

Your stomach tightens. Your breath catches. For a moment, your thoughts stall and scatter. In an instant, your brain starts preparing for every possible scenario, none of them good. And without realising it, you're already somewhere else. Not at your desk and definitely not focusing on dinner.

You're inside the churn of uncertainty.

This is exactly the kind of micro-moment where Autopilot takes over. It's nothing to do with intelligence or experience. It's about speed. When the pressure hits, your brain tries to protect you by reaching for whatever feels fast, familiar or safe.

It's the start of The Moment. And it's the point where you can choose to respond differently.

The four moves in action

Feel it: Tune in to your body's signal

You notice the change immediately. That subtle but undeniable internal jolt. The way your chest tightens and your thoughts speed up or shut down.

'Okay. That landed hard. I can feel it in my gut.'

Name it: Step back by externalising the state

Before the sensation pulls you into a spiral, you pause and put a name to it. You catch the swirl and mark it for what it is.

'Right. This is a messy moment. My brain is about to shift into reaction mode.'

Calm it: Downshift your nervous system to enable thinking

You interrupt the rising urgency. One steady breath. Feel your feet on the floor. A small but deliberate pause.

> *'This feels uncertain. But it is not danger. I don't need to solve anything right now.'*

Claim it: Choose curiosity over escaping discomfort

Here is where the shift happens. Instead of running from the discomfort, you decide to stay with it just for a moment longer. You resist the pull to guess, fix or worry it into submission.

> *'I have no idea what this is about, and I won't know until tomorrow. But I wonder what it could be. Maybe it's important. Maybe it isn't. Either way, I don't have to lose tonight to something I can't control. This evening still matters. I want to be here for it.'*

With those four small moves, you have caught The Moment. You didn't resolve anything or figure anything out. Instead, you did something more powerful. You created space. You stepped out of your reactive pattern and chose how to respond.

Like a surfer leaning into the wave, you balanced yourself and stayed with The Moment, rather than being swept away by it.

That is Activation and that... is where clarity begins.

THE POWER OF CHOICE

Activation doesn't magically resolve the complexity of the situation, instantly fix the underlying challenge or reveal the hidden answer.

It gives you something more fundamental - something essential for navigating everything that follows: choice.

More specifically, Activation gives you the choice to:

- notice instead of merely react.
- breathe and create space instead of bracing against discomfort.
- consciously decide how you want to engage your thinking, before jumping into 'what should I do?'

Most approaches to problem solving or decision-making in uncertainty skip past this crucial internal step.

They assume clarity comes from gathering more information, creating a logic tree or landing on the right answer *out there*. But in the face of complexity and uncertainty, real clarity starts on the *inside*. It begins with how you meet The Moment of disorientation, before an alternative path is clear and before an answer is even possible.

That's the key. Activation gives you back access to your thinking, right at the point where you're most likely to hand it over to habit, fear or the pull of urgency.

That's what makes Activation the first, foundational level of The Moment Method. It's not the most sophisticated, but because everything that comes after depends on getting this first step right.

When you start using the Moment Method, it's worth remembering: Activation doesn't mean executing these four moves perfectly every time - especially under pressure. It's about building the practice of presence and choice.

Each time you move through Feel, Name, Calm, Claim - even briefly, even imperfectly - you strengthen your brain's ability to catch the shift and respond deliberately, rather than sliding into Autopilot. And that capacity becomes most valuable when the stakes are highest.

And now that you've used Activation to create that essential space - emotionally, cognitively and physiologically - your brain is ready for what comes next.

Namely, Mastery Level 2 in the Moment Method: **Articulate**.

MAKE IT REAL

This chapter has covered a lot of ground and now you have the opportunity to put some of this thinking into practice. I recommend that you take your time and start by just noticing what's going on.

Notice what happens to your thinking when someone asks you a question.

_____

_____

_____

Notice something unexpected happens at work or home and see if you can catch The Moment.

_____

_____

_____

Notice the conversations between other people. Where does The Moment show up and does anything change as a result or do things simply power straight ahead?

_____

_____

_____

Key takeaway:

The Moment Method is a practice. The more you do it, the easier it becomes. No one is there marking your performance, so in the coming days and weeks, test it out. You'll be surprised how quickly it becomes second nature.

CHAPTER IN A NUTSHELL

- Activation is the first move in breaking free from The Answer Trap - it creates space between trigger and reaction.

- It begins when you notice a subtle internal shift: tension, blankness, urgency or hesitation - the early signal of a messy moment.

- Without Activation, the brain defaults to fast relief, pulling you into Autopilot before conscious thinking can begin.

- Activation interrupts this reflex with four deliberate moves: Feel it, Name it, Calm it, Claim it.

- It's not about stopping every reaction - it's about noticing when a moment matters and choosing how to engage.

- You don't need to catch it early - you just need to catch it. Every moment of awareness is an opportunity to take back control.

- Activation doesn't try to address the situation - it gives you the power to lead your thinking, instead of being led by it.

CHAPTER 13
ARTICULATE

Have you ever noticed how, when you're feeling stuck or over-whelmed, your brain grabs the first question it can find?

And then, like a whirlpool, you spin around it again and again, hoping the answer will eventually pull you out.

I met up with a friend of mine recently, Angela, who'd been caught in exactly that kind of mental current. She's brilliant, hugely experienced, the kind of person everyone respects. But she was navigating a tough career transition.

ANGELA'S STORY

Months had gone by. Countless coffees, endless networking conversations, plenty of interviews. Yet nothing solid was landing. She felt adrift, frustrated and increasingly disillusioned.

The question looping relentlessly in Angela's head felt entirely logical:

'How do I get a job?'

It looked like the obvious target. The problem seemed to be unemployment, so the answer must be employment. It gave her brain something concrete to work on. A direction to paddle in.

But the longer she stayed in that question, the more stuck she became. Caught in its spin, unable to surface. And the more she wrestled with it, the heavier it felt.

Every polite rejection and every promising lead that fizzled out just fed the negative loop. *'Why can't I get this right? What's wrong with me?'*

Worse, she realised with a jolt, she didn't even feel real disappointment when she missed out. It was a telling sign that something fundamental was off.

One day, smack bang in the middle of yet another dead-end networking conversation, something inside her just cracked. She stopped talking. Stopped trying. And this thought landed, quietly and clearly:

'I don't even know if I want this anymore.'

Crucially, she noticed this internal shift. That pause where the old script and the old questions just fell away?

Whether she consciously labelled it or not, she had Activated *The Moment* and created space.

She was sitting there, in The Moment, right on the edge between grabbing the familiar, unhelpful question ('How do I get a job?') and shaping one that actually mattered to her.

And in that space, instead of immediately chasing the nearest answer, she let a different kind of question surface. One focused not on external validation, but on internal alignment:

'What do I actually want?'

In doing this, Angela Articulated her moment. She reframed it, replacing the old unhelpful questions with one that gave her brain a real job to do. It was a meaningful puzzle to work on that started pulling her towards genuine clarity instead of just spinning her more deeply.

From that point forward, everything began to shift.

Angela stopped reacting to every job alert. She stopped forcing herself through applications for roles that didn't resonate. She stopped trying to contort herself to fit conversations and psych evaluations that were clearly going nowhere useful.

Instead, she started exploring, deliberately, thoughtfully, what she actually wanted her next chapter to look like, feel like, and be about. What mattered to her, not just what looked good on paper or paid the bills.

That's the profound impact of Articulating The Moment.

> *Angela's experience highlights the insidious nature of the trap. Before our brain even gets close to an answer, it often locks onto a question.*

It's one that feels urgent, maybe even practical, like Angela's 'How do I get a job?', but it isn't actually the one that holds the key to meaningful progress.

When you Articulate well, you stop scrambling to escape the discomfort. You start thinking. Purposefully engaging with the uncertainty. And, as Angela described it, you feel an immense sense of relief, 'the lightest I've ever felt,' as the weight of the wrong expectations falls away.

In doing so, you start to take back control of your own thinking.

WHY ARTICULATE?

Angela's shift from frustration to focused exploration underscores why in The Moment Method, Articulation is the crucial next step after Activation.

Once you've deliberately stepped into that turbulent, unstable space, your brain isn't designed to just hang out comfortably in ambiguity. The instant you create that pause, it starts searching, sometimes frantically, for something solid to grab onto and work on.

Your brain craves focus. *'Just give me something to do'*.

If you don't consciously give your brain a meaningful task in that activated Moment, it will invent one. And that self-assigned task is almost always aimed at ending the discomfort of 'not knowing' as fast as possible. This is how we drift back into reactive patterns even after successfully Activating and it's where Articulation comes in.

It's about deliberately shaping the structure and focus within that space you created. When you Articulate, instead of letting your brain drift back into default reactions, you consciously design the Critical Question for this moment.

Angela's Critical Question was *'What do I really want?'*

So, what happened next?

This shift in thinking completely changed her approach. Instead of chasing every lead and forcing herself into roles that didn't fit, she redirected her energy towards conversations and opportunities that actually aligned with what mattered to her.

This led to a remarkable turning point.

Six months earlier, Angela had been invited to apply for a role that she turned down. At the time, it didn't fit the version of success her Autopilot was chasing. She said no because it didn't match what she thought she *should* want.

But with her Critical Question guiding her, that same opportunity now looked completely different. This time, it felt like home.

As Angela described it, 'that darn Autopilot' had steered her towards the expected path, not the meaningful one. Once she broke that pattern, she saw the value-aligned opportunity for what it truly was.

Today, she's thriving in the role. She feels deeply connected to the purpose of her work. And, in her own words 'for the first time in a long time, experiences real joy from what she does'.

A good Critical Question creates what I call 'cognitive gravity'.

If Activation stops the uncontrolled spinning, Articulation identifies the specific point that you want your thinking to orbit around.

This question acts like an anchor, exerting a gentle but firm pull that draws our brain's energy towards meaningful engagement and away from panicked reacting or drifting back into old habits.

The Critical Question gives our brain the clear, compelling task it needs to stay grounded in the uncertainty, long enough to think usefully.

Without this step consciously setting the thinking task, we often leave a vacuum.

Articulation prevents that drift and sets the agenda for your thinking, before Autopilot does it for you.

THE MISTAKE THAT'S EASY TO MAKE

Now, needing focus is one thing, but grabbing the wrong focus is where things go sideways rapidly. So, here's an important issue to watch out for.

Sometimes, we hit pause, we know we need a Critical Question but instead of consciously designing it, we often grab the first one that pops into our head.

It's a default reaction, masquerading as
deliberate thinking.

Frequently, that default question is often some variation of this:

- 'What's the problem to be solved?'

It sounds sensible, right? Practical. Action oriented.

It's not that it's a bad question. However, locking onto this question too quickly, as the primary focus, can oversimplify the situation and blind us to what really matters. It subtly steers us towards three unhelpful paths.

- **Adopting a negative lens**

  Moments are neither negative nor positive. They are neutral. So, when our Critical Question labels The Moment 'a problem' we signal to our brain that the situation is negative. This closes off our cognitive options, stops us looking for the opportunity and leaves the door open to our Autopilot.

- **Binary thinking**

  Is there a problem (yes/no)? Can we fix it (yes/no)? Complexity gets squeezed into simple, often inaccurate boxes that ignore nuances and interdependencies. And unwittingly, we attach ourselves to Solving mode, even when other thinking modes are needed.

- **Solving over understanding**

  The rush to 'fix' bypasses deeper exploration of context, the needs or underlying dynamics.

You know? There's a feeling and I reckon you've probably experienced it.

It's the feeling of working incredibly hard on a solution, maybe even delivering it successfully, only to realise later that it didn't address the real, underlying issue?

My CoronaCommunities project during the pandemic, that never got off the ground, is a classic example.

That sinking feeling is often the result of brilliantly, diligently answering a default question like 'What's the problem?' without first pausing to ask if that was the right question to begin with for this specific moment.

This danger becomes even more pronounced when we try to navigate moments *together*, as the following example illustrates.

THE SOLAR PANEL SCENARIO

Imagine that you and your partner are discussing solar panels. The obvious question seems to be, 'Should we get them?' But after a while you find yourselves talking in circles, no closer to a resolution.

Why?

Because while you're both using the same words, you might be trying to address different underlying contexts, driven by different needs.

Remember our earlier discussion about your brain trying to help you make progress, by getting you from Point A to Point B? Point A is 'where you are' and Point B is 'where you want to be'.

This helps to show why creating your Critical Question is so important. Let's apply it to the solar panel conversation.

OUT IN THE OPEN		INSIDE YOUR HEADS			
The spoken question		A Where you are	Disruption that triggers The Moment	B Where you want to be	The unspoken question
YOU	'Should we get solar panels?'	Paying more for power	Rising cost of electricity	Paying less for power	'How can we slash our energy bills?'
PARTNER		High risk of power loss	Lost power in a flood	Low risk of power loss	'How can we guarantee power for essentials during an emergency?'

First, consider your perspective.

Perhaps your main concern is the rising cost of electricity. Therefore, your personal Point A to B might be moving from paying more for power to paying less for it. In your head, the unspoken question you might therefore be answering in the conversation is really, 'How can we slash our energy bills?'

Your partner, however, might be focused on recent floods and power outages; their underlying need might be to move from what they consider to be a high risk of power loss to being a low risk, especially in natural disasters. Your partner's unspoken question might be: 'How can we guarantee power for essentials during an emergency?'

See the difference?

On the surface, you both think you're answering the *spoken* question 'Should we get solar panels?'. But when thinking about the answer, your brains are each answering different questions, based on different points A and B.

You both think that you've Activated The Moment by sitting down to talk. Yet, you've actually Activated two separate Moments while *assuming* you're in the same one.

To move forward together, you both need to shift your attention from the spoken question, to the unspoken one. Then, Articulate a shared Critical Question, one that acknowledges both needs. Perhaps it's something like:

- *'What power solution best minimises our costs while ensuring emergency reliability?'*

Only by taking the time to Articulate that shared question first and having a conversation to align behind that, can you determine if solar panels are the right answer for both of you. And, if they are, why they are the right answer and how you'll measure success.

When you're in The Moment, the answer only makes sense once you know the Critical Question.

That's why we Articulate: not to overcomplicate things unnecessarily, but to clarify what this Moment is really about for us. Whether it's a solo Moment or one that is shared with others, the biggest trap isn't getting the answer wrong. Often, it's answering the wrong question: brilliantly.

But let's expand this even further and look at how Articulation plays out when teams and even organisations are sharing the same Moment.

MARIO'S MOMENT

One of my clients, Mario, was grappling with the full weight of disruption.

His industry was shifting rapidly. Customer expectations were evolving, the market was volatile and internally, his team was contending with restructuring and strategy pivots that left everyone feeling off balance.

Despite his years of experience, Mario felt stuck. As he put it, 'It's like we're trapped in the perfect storm. Nothing's stable. Even the things that used to work don't anymore. And when I try to make sense of it all, my brain goes on strike.'

Instead of answers, all I get are more questions.'

Mario had been asked to lead the rollout of a new commercial strategy - one that aimed to deliver a twenty percent increase in revenue without any increase in budget. In response, he'd organised a three-day off-site for his leadership team. The plan was to reconnect people, rebuild energy and get aligned on execution. On the surface, it was a logical move.

But when we started unpacking it, something didn't sit right.

The more we explored, the clearer it became that the real issue wasn't how to execute the strategy - it was how the strategy itself had been framed. The Moment wasn't actually about alignment. It was about meaning.

Rather than dive into the logistics of the off-site, I asked Mario: *'What's the big question this strategy is actually answering?'*

He hesitated. 'I guess it's: how do we achieve a twenty percent increase in sales with the same budget?'

Then I asked: *'And how does that question make you feel?'*

He didn't even pause. 'Exhausted. Overwhelmed. Frustrated.'

That moment mattered.

> *If the question guiding the entire strategy made the person leading it feel drained and boxed in, what chance did his team have of feeling engaged by it?*

The question they were holding - quietly, implicitly - wasn't one that inspired creativity or forward momentum. It was one that reinforced pressure, constraint and urgency. Even the off-site itself risked becoming a space where everyone scrambled for short-term fixes, instead of asking what The Moment really required.

So, we stepped back. Paused. And together, Mario and I reframed The Moment.

Instead of focusing on 'How do we hit the number without spending more?' we landed on a different, more deliberate, question:

'How will we create so much value for current and future customers that they can't wait to join and never want to leave - while also achieving profitable growth?'

That one shift changed everything. It shifted the gravitational centre of the work. The energy in his thinking changed almost immediately - from internal pressure to external purpose. From constraint to creativity and from reactive problem-solving to genuine opportunity-finding.

With the new question in place, the off-site was completely redesigned. We'll come back to what happened there a bit later.

★★★

All of these examples illustrate how something that at first seems small and insignificant, makes a massive difference to the shape of The Moment you're in and the direction your thinking takes.

This brings us to the next logical question 'How do you articulate your moment?'

Interestingly, the first practical step is more about attitude than action.

RETHINK YOUR RELATIONSHIP WITH QUESTIONS

Learning to Articulate effectively starts with rethinking our entire relationship with questions. Most of us are so deeply conditioned by school, work and life to value *answers*. Knowing the answer is rewarded; not knowing, or asking questions that reveal uncertainty, can feel uncomfortable, even risky.

Somewhere along the line, we stop seeing questions primarily as powerful tools for exploration and discovery and start seeing them more like tests we might fail.

Think about your own experience. Have you ever been asked a question, in public, that you didn't know the answer to? Was that an experience you'd like to repeat again soon?

I'm guessing, but probably not, right?

We'll talk a lot more about the power of questions in the next chapter. For now, however, take a moment to consider your re-lationship with questions, particularly those for which you don't have an answer.

MAKE IT REAL

In the coming days, notice the questions you ask, either out loud or in your head.

What is the intention behind the question?

_____

_____

Why is the question being asked?

_____

_____

How does it feel when you ask an important question, but don't get an answer?

_____

_____

Also, take note of the questions that are asked of you. What is the intention behind those questions?

_____

_____

Why are those questions being asked?

_____

_____

How do you feel when you do or don't have the answer from someone who matters to you?

_____

_____

Key takeaway:

The range of questions we ask and are asked, is often narrow. Their goal is to find out things that we want to know. Or to test others regarding what *they* know.

Yet, when it comes to thinking, questions have an extraordinary range of possible applications. They are like a cognitive multi-tool - one of those huge Swiss army knives you take camping. When you think of them this way, it starts to change your relationship with them.

THREE WAYS TO DESIGN THE QUESTION THAT MATTERS

How do you actually *find* that Critical Question, the one that creates useful cognitive gravity and focuses your thinking effectively in The Moment?

It's definitely more art than science and it absolutely takes practice. But here are three distinct approaches that my clients find helpful when they're navigating this crucial step.

Think of these as different ways into the same challenge: designing the question that truly matters right now. You don't need to do all three every time; often one is enough to unlock things.

1. Match effort with intent

Our brains love the feeling of momentum, especially under pressure and will often just take off down the nearest runway without double checking the intended destination. This strategy forces that crucial pause to ensure your actions align with your real purpose.

How:

When you feel that sense of being incredibly busy but maybe directionless, working hard but feeling vaguely off track, pause.

- **Ask yourself honestly:** 'Setting aside the tasks for a minute, what goal is my brain actually racing towards right now with all this effort?'
- **Try to name the implied destination** or outcome it's chasing. Then, assess with brutal honesty:

  - 'Is this really the most important destination for me right now?
  - Is this the flight I truly need to be on, or am I just hurtling down this familiar runway because movement feels better than stillness, or because it's the path expected of me?'

- If you realise you've got the wrong flight plan, give yourself permission to stop, even if you're already accelerating.
- Use the pause to consciously design the Critical Question that sets the *right* destination for *this* leg of your journey.

Try it:

Next time you feel that surge of busyness, especially if it feels a bit reactive or driven by external pressure, take 30 seconds.

- **Ask yourself:** *'Is this flight plan still valid and truly mine, or am I just moving because I feel I should?'* Better to pause on the tarmac and recalibrate than realise halfway across the ocean you're headed somewhere you don't want to be.

2. Question the question

This strategy is about developing the reflex to catch your brain in the very act of grabbing its default, often reactive, question. Remember how quickly it latches onto *something* in a moment of pressure – often a familiar query like 'How do I fix this?' or 'How do I win this argument?' or 'How do I make this discomfort stop?'

This strategy challenges that first, automatic question directly.

How:

When you notice yourself starting to spin mentally, react defensively or feel that intense pressure for an immediate answer, stop.

- **Ask yourself:** 'Okay, hold on. What question is my brain already trying to answer here, maybe automatically, under the surface?'

- **Don't overthink it;** just try to name the implicit task it's grabbed onto. Say it out loud if it helps. Then, get genuinely curious: *'Is this question actually helping me stay steady and think clearly right now? Is it leading me towards useful insight, or is it just fuelling the reactive scramble?'* If it feels like the latter, consciously reframe it, right there on the spot.

- **Shift from the reactive default** to a question that feels more grounded, more exploratory, more useful for *this* moment. For example, *'How do I fix this?'* might become *'What needs my most careful attention right now?'* *'How do I prove I'm right?'* could shift to *'What's most important for me/us to understand here?'*

You'll often feel a subtle easing of internal tension when you land on a more constructive, less reactive question. You regain a sense of control over your thinking process.

Try it:

When you feel that internal pressure cooker start hissing, pause.

- **Ask:** 'What's the question driving this pressure? Is it the right one for this Moment?' If not, take a breath and redesign it.

It's truly amazing how consciously changing the question you're holding can change the entire feeling and direction of your thinking.

3. Get to the heart of The Moment

This third approach often goes a bit deeper. It's concerned with consciously designing your Critical Question by first trying to identify the core 'lever' in the situation. It's that central element, tension or underlying need that, if you could just grasp or shift it, would change your perspective on everything else. This involves getting beneath the surface noise and identifying the crux of the matter *for you, right now.*

How:

- **Ask yourself:** 'Setting aside the immediate symptoms and distractions, what's the real heart of this situation for me?'

  - What's the core tension I'm feeling, the underlying need that's not being met? Or, what's the central point that, if I focused on it, would bring the most clarity or unlock the most useful thinking?'

- Is the lever about achieving *clarity* itself? Or is it about taking *ownership*? Finding *meaning*? Strengthening *connection*? Establishing *boundaries*?

- **Try to sense what feels most central**. Once you have a hunch about the lever, then you craft the Critical Question specifically designed to engage directly with that. For instance:

  - If the lever feels like needing **Clarity**, the Critical Question might be: *'What's really going on beneath the surface here?'*
  - If it feels like **Ownership**, perhaps: 'What is mine and only mine, to do in this situation right now?'
  - If it's about **Meaning**, maybe: 'What truly matters most to me in how this unfolds?'

The goal is to design *one focused question* that creates that cognitive gravity around the lever you've identified, pulling your thinking towards the heart of The Moment.

HOW YOU'LL KNOW YOU'VE LANDED IT

Landing your Critical Question often brings a distinct feeling of 'groundedness'. The internal noise might quieten. Your brain stops frantically scrambling and seems to lean *in*, interested.

It doesn't always feel like instant relief, but more like your feet hitting solid earth after slipping. Sometimes you'll physically want to write it down, to capture it. That's often a sign you've found your anchor.

The three strategies we just discussed aren't a rigid sequence to be followed every time. They're different angles of attack, different tools you can use depending on the situation, to achieve the same goal. That is, moving beyond reactive default questions to consciously designing the *one* Critical Question that provides the gravity you need for *this* specific Moment.

BUILD THE MENTAL MUSCLE

There are many ways to Articulate your Critical Question.

The thing to remember is to keep asking and answering questions that encourage different modes of thinking. Exploring, Learning, Sensemaking and so on. Eventually, an answer will resonate more than the others. Notice it. Then, you can use that question as your base for the next set of questions.

But, if you're just starting out, what else can you do to make it easier?

Practice in the low-stakes moments

Reading about these approaches is one thing; actually using them when the pressure hits is another. The key isn't to suddenly become a master question-designer overnight, especially not in your most high-stakes situations.

Trying to learn a new, complex skill when you're already stressed is like trying to learn advanced calculus during the final exam. It's not usually effective!

> *The real trick to getting good at Articulation is to practice consistently where the stakes are low. Build the muscle memory in the everyday.*

That's how this concept evolves from being just an interesting idea in a book, to becoming an intuitive skill you can reliably draw upon when things get really complex. The more you practise finding your anchor in the small waves, the more readily and skilfully you'll find it when the big ones roll in.

MAKE IT REAL

Next time you feel even a small internal wobble - a slight confusion during a routine meeting, a flicker of frustration reading an email, a moment of uncertainty about what task to tackle next - see it as a practice opportunity. Pause briefly (Activate). Then immediately ask yourself:

'What question is my brain defaulting to right now?'

_____

_____

_____

'Is there a simple lever here - what's really bothering me or what do I really need?'

_____

_____

_____

'What's one slightly better question I could ask myself right now to feel more focused or clear, even just for the next ten minutes?'

_____

_____

_____

Key takeaway:

You don't need to have a profound breakthrough every time you practise. You're simply building the neural pathways, noticing your own default patterns and rehearsing the act of consciously choosing your focus, even for just a few minutes.

THE SHIFT STARTS RIGHT HERE

Have you ever been in a conversation where someone asked a question that made people pause and say 'Wow... that's a great question!'? Not because it provided the solution, but because it reframed the situation, surfaced a hidden assumption or opened up a pathway that no one had seen before?

That's the power we're tapping into when we Articulate.

Begin to see questions not just as requests for information, but as potent tools for shaping thought.

The right question, asked at the right time, doesn't just seek an answer; it creates focus, directs attention, shifts energy and opens up new possibilities.

Most importantly, it gives you a way to step into and engage with The Fog of Uncertainty.

Finding your Critical Question, your anchor point, is crucial to reach Mastery Level 2 in The Moment Method. But just having the anchor isn't enough; you still need to navigate the waters around it.

- How do you actually *work* with that Critical Question once you've found it?

- How do you explore the territory it opens up without getting lost again, without prematurely rushing for the relief of an easy answer and without falling back into old Autopilot habits?

- How do you stay in the productive tension of the question long enough to find genuine insight and chart a path towards useful momentum?

That's the art of deliberate thinking in action. And that's precisely where we're headed next, into Mastery Level 3 in the Moment Method: **Navigate.**

CHAPTER IN A NUTSHELL

- After Activation creates space, your brain urgently seeks focus - if you don't shape that focus, Autopilot will.

- Articulation is the act of designing a Critical Question that creates cognitive gravity and anchors your thinking in uncertainty.

- Default questions often seek relief, not clarity - leading you to answer the wrong question brilliantly.

- By consciously shaping the question that matters, you interrupt drift and set your brain a task worth doing.

- There are three powerful ways in: Match effort with intent, Question the question, Get to the heart of The Moment.

- Practising in low-stakes moments builds your ability to hold steady when the pressure's high.

- Great questions don't just seek answers - they change the way you think. That's how you escape The Answer Trap and reclaim control.

CHAPTER 14
NAVIGATE

We've reached the final chapter of Part 3, and you've already achieved something most people never even notice, let alone master.

You've Activated The Moment instead of defaulting to Autopilot, and you've Articulated the Critical Question – the one that truly matters.

So, there you are, standing in the mess, holding that question in your mind like a fragile compass. You've made it... right?

Not quite.

Here's the challenge that no one really warns you about.

The moment you land on your Critical Question, even a brilliant one, your brain often exhales with a subtle 'Phew... we're done.' It feels like a finish line, a flicker of relief as if clarity is complete.

But what's really happening?

Your brain, true to its design to conserve energy and seek closure, is already looking for the nearest exit.

Yes, again!

It's not weakness or a lack of discipline; it's your brain doing its job. Yet, this very efficiency is what makes Navigate so challenging. It's not that this stage is more intellectually complex than Activation or Articulation. It's that it asks you to do something profoundly counter-intuitive: it asks you to *stay*.

To resist that powerful pull towards premature closure and hold your ground. Not with gritted teeth or brute force, but with deliberate, curious engagement. And that—holding your question and continuing to *work* it when every instinct is screaming for the comfort of an answer—that's the hardest step of all.

WHERE THINKING BECOMES DOING

This is Navigate. It's the third level of The Moment Method, where consciously *working* your Critical Question transforms thinking into the actual doing. This is *the real work* of making progress in complexity.

We're deeply conditioned to see thinking as mere preparation: the planning phase, the prelude, the prep, but not the main event. Typically, we do just enough of it to enable us to act. Then, we stop.

But in moments of real complexity, that belief that thinking is 'pre-work' will fail you.

In these moments - where the stakes are high, the clarity is low and there's no obvious path forward - thinking IS the work.

The sustained, deliberate process of staying with your question, shaping your attention and nudging your mind forward through the fog... that *is* the action. That's what makes the next step, the one out of The Moment, possible. It's not passive or overthinking. It's purposeful engagement.

This is what Navigate asks of you: that you work your question, rather than rush to answer it, and allow your thinking to move – gently, deliberately – even while the outcome remains uncertain. Your brain is 'dancing with disruption'.

The thinking modes are like a set of possible dance moves, but you don't know which one you'll use until you're on the dance floor. You have to pay attention and constantly adjust to where you are in The Moment.

Sometimes this means shifting your focus slightly. Other times it means asking a different kind of question or recognising that you're in the fog and still choosing to stay alert inside it. You're not waiting for clarity to strike like lightning. Instead, you're creating it – one useful thought at a time.

So, in this chapter, we need to get honest about what pulls us away from this kind of thinking. Why it's hard to stay and why our brains resist. And then, most importantly, how we train ourselves to remain in The Moment long enough to let clarity emerge.

That's where we turn next.

STEERING YOUR THINKING WITH QUESTIONS

Once you've chosen to stay in The Moment and committed to working the question rather than escaping it, your next challenge isn't just to hold the question. It's to keep thinking in a way that actually helps you move.

And here's the bit we often miss: the way your brain thinks is shaped by the question it believes it's trying to answer.

You saw this in the Solar Panel Scenario in the previous chapter. That's what determines which mode of thinking kicks in.

If the question you're asking is *'What's the problem here?'* your brain naturally drops into Solving mode.

If it's *'What haven't we considered yet?'* you're likely to engage Exploring mode. If you're asking *'What should I do next?'*, you're shifting into Doing mode, whether the situation needs action or not.

Your brain is responding to the job it thinks you've given it, based on the question you're holding in your head.

Recall the Solar Panel scenario again and the unspoken questions that you and your partner defaulted to.

In that example, *your* brain (representing one partner's perspective) likely saw its job as addressing the monetary pain of increasing power prices. This would lead to your default, unspoken question: 'How can we slash our energy bills?'

Similarly, *your partner's* brain saw its job differently, focusing on reducing the physical risk of power blackouts in an emergency. This naturally led to their unspoken question: 'How can we guarantee power for essentials during an emergency?'

Two distinct unspoken questions, both potentially defaulting your thinking to *Solving mode* but crucially, motivated by different underlying needs.

Your brains were dancing with two different disruptions (price increases and floods), so your heads were never going to be in the same dance or even on the same dance floor.

That's how easily you can find yourselves working hard, thinking hard, and still not feeling like you're making progress *together*. It's often a mode mismatch, or a mismatch of the needs being addressed, and… it happens all the time.

This is where deliberate thinking begins.

When you can recognise which mode your question is initiating - and choose to shift it - you change the way your brain engages.

You give it a better task. A more useful job. And in doing so, you make it possible to stay in the complexity without shutting down or jumping too quickly to the nearest answer.

So, how do you do that in practice? How do you stay curious, focused and steady - without defaulting back to Autopilot?

That's where we go next. It's a skill that I call Questioneering.

QUESTIONEERING: THE ULTIMATE SKILL FOR A DISRUPTED WORLD

You've named your Critical Question. But what now? How do you actually *work* that question in a way that generates clarity and momentum?

This is where most people drift, because they've never been taught a practical way to stay with the Critical Question and use it deliberately to guide their thinking.

That's why I developed Questioneering.

Creating clarity in complexity

Questioneering is a structured practice for navigating complexity through the intentional use of questions. It goes beyond just asking *more* questions or asking *a different type* of questions. It's about designing and sequencing questions to enable your thinking to shift effectively between different modes and move you through The Moment.

The name itself is designed to capture the core elements of this skill:

- **Quest:** You're on a purposeful journey of exploration, guided by your Critical Question. This isn't random inquiry; it's a focused quest for deeper understanding.

- **Pioneering:** You're venturing into new mental territory, exploring possibilities and perspectives beyond the obvious. You're pioneering new pathways through the challenge.

- **Engineering:** You're consciously designing questions with precision, crafting them as tools to achieve specific cognitive aims. This is cognitive engineering, not passive curiosity.

- **The 'ion':** Like ions in chemistry, quest-ions carry a cognitive charge, an energy that can shift your attention, re-energise your thinking and create movement when your brain wants to settle.

Finding a foothold

Using Questioneering to navigate The Moment is a bit like taking on a challenging rock climb.

Each possible question you could ask is like a potential handhold or foothold on the entire rock face. You don't have to select every single one that The Moment throws at you. Just the useful ones that help you progress.

So, how do you tell the useful questions from the others? Here's where the climbing analogy really helps.

Let's imagine you're an experienced rock-climbing enthusiast. It's a beautiful summer's day and you're right there - thirty metres up a rock face you've never climbed before. You need to make your next move.

How would you do that?

Well, you'd probably start by assessing the handholds and footholds within your immediate reach. Of those, you'd likely go for the ones that look most secure and, ideally, help you move upwards.

Conversely, you wouldn't lunge for a distant ledge simply because it's higher up, if it meant an overly risky or impossible move. Sometimes the best next step might even be sideways, or a slight retreat to find a more viable path forward if you can't advance directly from where you are.

Questioneering works in much the same way.

Your Critical Question becomes the cliff face you're scaling, and Questioneering provides the method to navigate that climb, one deliberate question—one secure foothold—at a time.

You target a question—a potential foothold—and attempt to answer it. This is like a climber making a deliberate move from their current position to that chosen hold. When you reach an answer, you've successfully made that move and established a new position, a new vantage point on the cliff face.

You now know more and have a fresh perspective.

From this new position, the process of identifying and targeting your next useful question continues, step by step, until you reach the other side of The Moment.

The key is to avoid lunging for a distant, perhaps overwhelming final answer. Instead, like the climber, you continually look for the *next useful question*. This question is useful because it's grounded in your Critical Question, where you ultimately want to be, and, crucially, where you *actually are* in your understanding right now— not where you assumed you'd be.

Therefore, the most effective next question is almost always the one 'closest' to you: it's answerable from your current vantage point.

Why Questioneering works

Reaching for a closer, useful question is powerful because of what it does for your brain.

When we select a manageable, answerable question, we significantly reduce the risk our brain perceives. This, in turn, lessens the reactive urge that tries to pull us into Autopilot and helps take the fear out of the unknown.

Instead of your brain scrambling for an escape route from the discomfort of The Moment, it becomes engaged in the more constructive task of finding and working the next, achievable question.

And here's a crucial insight into the power of Questioneering. The perceived risk is lower so your brain can genuinely relax.

When it's not on high alert, it becomes significantly more open and adept at moving fluidly between different thinking modes, as the situation demands, rather than being locked into a single, often defensive, response.

Sometimes, as with climbing, you may need to backtrack or adopt a different perspective on the same topic to find a new, answerable question that enables you to move forward.

That's the work. You move with intention, looking for the questions that sit beneath your Critical Question, the ones that act as your next secure hold. This continues until you have so much clarity that you can finally answer your Critical Question. And this signals the end of The Moment. It's what I mean when I say 'working the question.'

Just as you rarely know what the whole path up the cliff looks like from the start, the one that takes you from one side of The Moment to the other is never predetermined. It can't be planned in advance and instead, needs to be Navigated in real time. But even so, you learn to identify and take the next deliberate step.

Not every move goes directly upward.

Sometimes you shift sideways to find a better grip; sometimes you pause, stretch, or even retreat slightly to see a new route. That's not failure. It's skilful navigation.

That's how clarity is created in complexity.

GETTING STARTED

When learning Questioneering, the Launch, Orbit, Land framework offers a great starting point. Here's how it works.

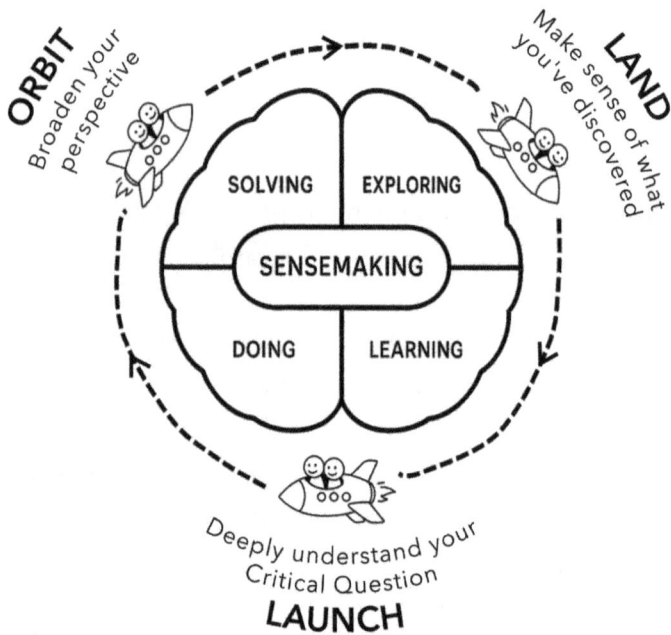

Launch: Begin by deeply understanding your Critical Question. Ask questions about the question itself:

- *What's this question truly about? What's its core?*

- *Why is it so important to answer this question right now? What's at stake?*

- *What assumptions might be influencing how I see it?*

Orbit: Systematically explore the situation by asking targeted questions that shift your thinking mode and broaden your perspective. For example:

- *Exploring: 'What's another way I could frame this situation?'*

- *Solving: 'What's the biggest obstacle preventing me from gaining clarity here?'*

- *Learning: 'What crucial information or insight am I currently missing?'*

- *Doing: 'What's one small experiment I could run to test this idea?'*

- *Sensemaking: 'What larger patterns are emerging as I consider this from different angles?'*

Land: Pause regularly to reflect and make sense of what you've discovered, adjusting your course as needed. Ask:

- *What feels clearer now than it did before?*

- *Has my understanding of the Critical Question evolved or deepened?*

- *What's the most useful thinking mode to engage with next?*

This Launch, Orbit, Land process isn't a rigid, one-time sequence. You'll likely move back and forth between thinking modes, re-visiting earlier orbits or refining your initial launch, as you work through the complexity of the situation.

The key is to use questions with intention and ask the ones you can answer first. Then, guide your thinking to build clarity and momentum, one deliberate foothold at a time.

MAKE IT REAL

Think about the Critical Question you developed in the previous chapter (or come up with a new one if you'd prefer). How might you use the Launch - Orbit – Land approach.

What is a possible Launch question?

_____

_____

_____

Try answering it. Then, based on the answer, what Orbit question could you ask?

_____

_____

_____

Answer that question. Finally, what Landing question could you ask now?

_____

_____

_____

And repeat, based on where you are now.

Key takeaway:

The key is to use questions with intention, one at a time. Ask the ones you can answer first. Then, guide your thinking to build clarity and momentum, one deliberate foothold at a time.

Questioneering isn't some innate talent reserved for a select few. It's a learnable skill that's easy to start and improves with practice.

- You've seen how different questions fuel specific thinking modes.

- You've recognised how your Autopilot tries to pull you back to familiar (but maybe unhelpful) loops.

- You've learnt how Questioneering, using the Launch, Orbit, Land flow, provides a structured yet flexible way to keep your thinking constructive and moving forward.

We're nearing the end of Part 3, and we've covered considerable ground. But how do the three levels of The Moment Method fit together? And importantly, what does that look like in the real world?

Let's take a look.

MASTERING THE MOMENT IN REAL TIME

We've spent the last few chapters breaking The Moment down - catching it, naming it and working it.

Activate. Articulate. Navigate.

Each of these moves is powerful on its own. But real momentum happens when they come together, enabling you to move through a messy moment in real time, without sliding back into The Answer Trap.

To illustrate this we're going to zoom out and watch what it actually looks like when someone applies these first three levels of mastery - not perfectly, but deliberately.

Alex masters The Moment

You've met Alex before, sitting at her desk back in Chapter 1. Smart. Capable. Running on empty.

But today... is a new day.

The morning starts like most others. Still too many tabs open, inbox pinging, brain already spinning before she's even sat down properly.

Her Autopilot has already kicked in. The question in her head is familiar: *What do I fix first?*

She's barely touched her coffee when it happens.

Thunk!

She knocks the cup over.

It's not just a splash – it's a chocolate laced, cappuccino flood. Across her desk, over her notes, creeping toward her laptop. Her hands react before her brain can catch up. *Paper towel, laptop lift, damage control.*

Crisis averted. But she doesn't sit down straight away. She stands there, hand still gripping the soggy paper, eyes on the screen.

Messages blinking. Emails stacking. A spreadsheet half-finished.

And something shifts. Then, Alex switches from Autopilot to Copilot.

Alex Activates

Not with a grand declaration – just a pause. A flicker of awareness that she's caught in the swirl. She doesn't dive back in. She doesn't answer the chaos. She stays still – just long enough to notice it.

Seriously, what am I doing?

She breathes. The swirl's still there, but something feels different. And then, the real question lands - softly but heavily:

Alex Articulates.

What am I actually here for?

It's not a task. Not something to add to the to-do list. The Critical Question that cuts to the job that really matters.

That's it - The Moment.

She doesn't have an answer - yet. But she knows she doesn't want to lose that question. So instead of diving straight back into her tasks, she grabs her phone, pushes her chair back and heads out to get another coffee - and a little space to think.

Alex Navigates (Launch-Orbit-Land)

Walking down the street, phone ignored, she lets the question breathe.

Okay... what does 'What am I really here for?' actually mean - in this job, in this moment?

Her brain starts working it. Not urgently, but honestly.

It's not just clearing my inbox fastest. Not just juggling projects to look capable. There has to be more substance.

It's about... creating value. But what kind of value actually matters to me?

Not just cost savings or project wins - although those count. It's deeper than that.

It's the kind of value people feel. Like when I'm not in the room - and someone mentions my name - and people nod.

A quiet nod that says: She gets it. She shows up. We trust her.

A nod that means: We're better because she's here.

That's it. That's what I'm here for. She reaches the café, orders without thinking. The goal feels sharper now.

So, if that's the kind of value I want to create... how am I actually doing that right now?

Pause. Honesty kicks in.

Honestly? I'm not. I'm reacting. Firing off answers. Ticking boxes. It looks like progress - but feels like guessing.

So, what's actually getting in the way?

She doesn't have to think long.

It's me. Me, stuck in the swirl. Trying to please everyone. Trying to guess what they need without ever asking.

That's what's dragging her under.

Okay. That's the lever. The guessing has to stop. I need to stop reacting. I need to start asking.

Alex emerges from The Moment

And just like that - the next moves form. Alex has the answer to her Critical Question. Now, she can get on with putting it into action.

- **Step 1:** Book time with Claira (her boss). Not to give an update - but to ask: What does value look like from your perspective? And how do you think I'm tracking?

- **Step 2:** Check in with each of her direct reports. Ask honestly: What do you need from me right now to do your best work? Where am I helpful - and where might I be getting in the way?

Back at her desk, nothing external has changed. The email count's the same. The fires are still smouldering, but the swirl doesn't own her anymore.

Why? Because now she has a new question, not just to think about, but to lead her thinking with:

Is this creating the kind of value that actually matters?

It's a new filter through which everything passes. And that question changes everything.

BEYOND INDIVIDUAL MASTERY

Mastering the Moment Method gives you the core toolkit for leading *yourself* through uncertain, ambiguous and complex situations. You now have a way to stay grounded, focused and deliberate when pressure hits.

That's how real individual momentum is built, not through frantic speed, but through focused, conscious thinking.

This marks the completion of our journey through the individual application of The Moment Method.

But what happens when the challenge isn't just navigating your own thoughts, but navigating complexity *with others*?

Being able to master your own moment is incredibly powerful.

It changes how you experience pressure, how you make decisions and how you show up.

Yet, individual clarity doesn't automatically translate into collective progress.

Often, the biggest hurdles lie in bridging the gap between minds, especially when faced with ambiguity and disruption.

Why do groups get stuck, even when individuals are capable? How do our individual patterns create collective friction?

That crucial shift – from mastering your moment individually to understanding the dynamics of collective thinking – is exactly where we're heading next.

In Part 4, we'll dissect the common traps that ensnare groups, dragging them into The Answer Trap. Then, we'll explore the practices that unlock shared momentum and cultivate environments for bigger, better thinking, together.

Let's keep going.

PART 4:

IGNITE GROUP MOMENTUM

ALIGN

ACCELERATE

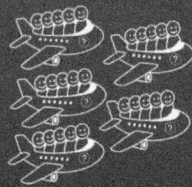

CULTIVATE

PART 4: WHAT TO EXPECT

You learnt the core moves of The Moment Method – how to **Activate** your awareness in the heat of The Moment, **Articulate** the Critical Question that truly matters and **Navigate** the often-uncomfortable space of uncertainty without defaulting back into The Answer Trap.

This ability to switch from Autopilot to Copilot is the essential foundation, a powerful capability in its own right.

But as anyone who works, lives or collaborates with other humans knows, what is clear to you, isn't always clear to others. And when we're in a disrupted environment, faced with unfamiliar and ambiguous situations, this gets worse.

Navigating complexity *together* presents a whole new layer of challenge.

Our individual Autopilots, assumptions and internal 'moments' can collide in ways that fragment focus and stall momentum, even when intentions are good. The very dynamics that trap us individually can create gridlock collectively. So:

- How do we bridge that gap?
- How do we move from managing our own thinking to fostering better thinking in others and together?
- How do we take the principles of The Moment Method and apply them not just within ourselves, but between us?

That crucial expansion is the focus of Part 4. Here, we shift our lens from the individual to the collective. We'll start by dissecting the common traps that ensnare groups. Then, we'll dive into **Accelerate**, exploring the art and practice of creating shared moments that ignite genuine shared momentum.

Finally, we'll look at **Cultivate**, considering how to embed these practices more deeply, nurturing environments where thoughtful, collaborative navigation becomes the norm, not the exception.

It's time to take the clarity you've learnt to build for yourself and explore how to help it ripple outwards. Let's begin by understanding why even the smartest groups can get stuck.

CHAPTER 15
WHY SMART GROUPS GET STUCK

Most of our important work, our most complex challenges, don't happen in isolation. We're constantly interacting, collaborating, deciding *with others*. In complexity, this is where things often get incredibly sticky, even when everyone involved is smart, capable and genuinely trying to move things forward.

Have you ever been in that meeting?

The one where everyone's talking, nodding, maybe even using the right buzzwords, whiteboards are filling up, actions seem to be assigned... but you have that nagging feeling deep down that you're all just spinning your wheels? And, that despite the appearance of activity, no real traction is being made on the thing that truly matters.

Or maybe you've left a meeting feeling like clear agreement was reached, only to find out later that people walked away with vastly different interpretations of what was decided, or what the *real* situation even was?

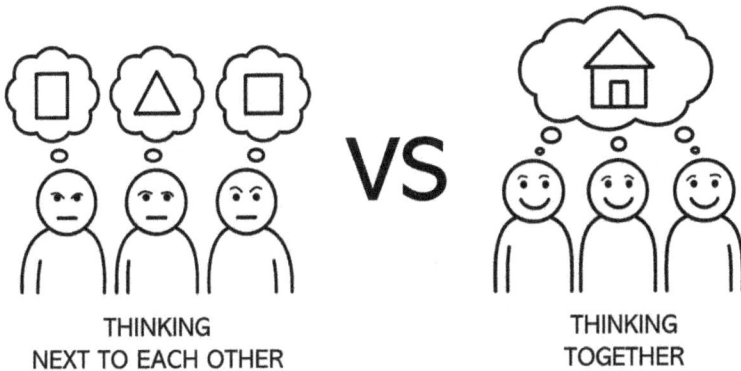

THINKING
NEXT TO EACH OTHER

VS

THINKING
TOGETHER

It's easy to assume that once a group agrees on something, they're aligned. But they're not the same.

Agreement usually forms around an *answer*. It sounds like progress, and it feels like closure, especially under pressure.

But alignment happens earlier. It's about whether we're holding the same *mental picture* of the situation: the priorities, constraints, stakes and success criteria. If that shared picture isn't in place, agreement becomes fragile. The moment pressure hits or plans shift, things start to unravel, because the group wasn't really thinking together in the first place.

This isn't just you.

It's an incredibly common experience in teams, organisations, even families. And it's deeply frustrating.

But why does this happen? Why do groups of intelligent, well-intentioned people so often fail to generate real, shared momentum?

It's usually not because of a lack of effort, commitment or even individual skill. The hidden culprit, more often than not, is *cognitive fragmentation*.

WHEN THINKING FRAGMENTS, PROGRESS BREAKS

While you might be diligently applying The Moment Method to navigate *your* internal experience, the person next to you is likely doing the same… but inside *their* own, slightly different version of The Moment.

Everyone ends up navigating their own internal landscape. They might be Activating at different times, Articulating subtly different Critical Questions based on their unique perspective or pressures and Navigating using different assumptions. Even if each person achieves individual clarity, that clarity isn't connected.

The Solar Panel Scenario was a good example of this. And the same thing happened to the Board members during that CEO crisis.

With everyone's Autopilots on board, it's like trying to get five talented people to jump effectively on the same trampoline when they're completely out of sync.

Each person's landing absorbs the energy from the others' jumps. Instead of using their combined force to launch higher together, they just flatten each other out.

Potential lift dissolves into a confusing jumble of competing forces. Activity replaces altitude. Noise replaces momentum.

That's cognitive fragmentation in action. When people aren't operating inside the same Moment:

- effort gets scattered.

- brilliant individual insights fail to connect or build.

- apparent agreement masks deep misalignment.

- momentum stalls, replaced by a feeling of wading through treacle.

- shared meaning erodes, leading to frustration and disengagement.

No single person is necessarily 'wrong' in their thinking. But the *collective* is stuck. They're not building shared understanding; they're inadvertently reinforcing their individual perspectives, making it even harder to find common ground.

And here's the crucial point: the more complex, ambiguous or high-pressure the situation, the *more* likely this fragmentation is to occur.

Just when we need cohesive thinking most, the conditions make it hardest to achieve.

So, what's driving this fragmentation at a deeper level?

It often comes down to our individual protective patterns kicking in automatically… then colliding.

WHEN AUTOPILOTS COLLIDE

We've already talked a lot about the Autopilots and how they aim to bring a sense of comfort or control when things feel uncertain. We've learnt how they can pull *us* into The Answer Trap individually.

Well, in a group setting, those same Autopilots become a major source of collective friction and inertia.

When a group hasn't consciously Activated a *shared* moment and Articulated a *shared* Critical Question, each person's brain, facing the ambiguity, tends to default to its preferred way of coping.

Their Autopilot takes the wheel to manage their *own* internal discomfort or drive towards *their* version of progress.

And suddenly, you have multiple Autopilots running simultaneously, often pulling in entirely different directions based on different underlying needs and assumptions:

- The **Driver** Autopilot, needing progress, starts pushing impatiently for *any* decision or action, potentially running over nuanced discussion. *'Okay, enough talk, what's the next step?'*

- The **Fact-Finder** Autopilot, craving certainty, stalls the process demanding more data or analysis, frustrating those ready to move. *'We can't decide yet; we still don't know X, Y and Z.'*

- The **Pioneer** Autopilot, seeking novelty, might start exploring radical alternatives or questioning the premise, while others are trying to solve the immediate, defined challenge. *'But what if we rethought the whole approach?'*

- The **Connector** Autopilot, prioritising intellectual and emotional cohesion, might focus on managing interpersonal dynamics or connecting the dots, sometimes avoiding necessary friction or slowing things down. *'Let's just make sure we're on the same page with this direction...'*

- The **Optimiser** Autopilot, needing precision, might get stuck refining a minor detail or process point, losing sight of the bigger picture or delaying progress. *'Before we move on, shouldn't we get this bit exactly right?'*

Again, none of these impulses are inherently bad. In the right context, each pattern brings value. But when they kick in *reactively*, driven by individual needs and aimed at resolving different internal tensions within an undefined Moment, they inevitably clash.

For example, what feels like:

- responsible action to the Driver, looks like recklessness to the Fact-Finder.

- necessary exploration to the Pioneer looks like distraction to the Optimiser.

- essential strategic thinking to the Connector looks like avoidance to the Driver.

And so, these mismatches go on. Not overtly where anyone can see them, but beneath the surface. They become part of *The Rip* and lead to three common consequences.

- **Cognitive clash:** Arguments over seemingly minor points because they represent different underlying assumptions.

- **Emotional drag:** Frustration, impatience, confusion, people feeling unheard or misunderstood. Trust can erode.

- **Stalled progress:** The group spins its wheels, unable to gain traction because the underlying forces are pulling it apart.

In groups, when decisions are driven by default Autopilot thinking, agreement becomes fragile.

It can only hold as long as things remain stable. The instant that pressure hits or the situation changes, or someone makes a call based on their own view of the world, decisions start to come apart.

And, because the divergent thinking was never visible to begin with, and usually happened a while ago, it's hard to name and address it.

In hindsight, those involved are often convinced that *they* saw the situation clearly and that *they* were acting rationally. They might also feel frustrated that *others* 'simply didn't get it'. And frequently, people assume this friction is personal.

Someone's resisting.

Someone's not listening.

Someone's going rogue.

But often, that *someone* was just answering a different version of the question, one they *thought* the group was asking.

And just like that, groups get pulled deeply into the collective Answer Trap: individually perhaps feeling clear or justified, but collectively, completely stuck.

Understanding this natural tendency towards cognitive fragmentation and the inevitable collision of Autopilots when a shared moment isn't established – is the crucial first step towards unlocking collective progress.

Recognising these patterns isn't about assigning blame; it's about diagnosing the hidden forces that keep smart groups from thinking effectively together – especially in turbulent times.

We've seen *why* shared momentum stalls and how easily individual clarity can fail to translate into group traction.

So, if fragmentation and colliding Autopilots are the problem, what's the solution? How do we counteract these dynamics?

Now that we've diagnosed *why* smart groups get stuck, we're ready to do something about it. In the next chapter, we'll dive into the practical heart of **Accelerate**: the art and practice of deliberately *activating*, *articulating* and *navigating* a shared Moment.

Join me as we take a closer look at Mastery Level 4 of the Moment Method.

CHAPTER IN A NUTSHELL

- Smart groups don't get stuck because people aren't contributing - they get stuck because their thinking isn't connected.

- Even smart, well-intentioned actions pull in different directions when driven by unaligned internal needs.

- In complexity, individual Autopilots activate simultaneously, each trying to create clarity - but without a shared moment, they collide.

- That's cognitive fragmentation: effort scatters, assumptions clash and momentum stalls.

- The messier The Moment, the more likely this happens - just when we need cohesion most.

- Recognising fragmentation isn't about blame - it's the first step to unlocking shared progress.

- And the key is this: Until we create a shared moment, we'll stay stuck in the collective Answer Trap.

CHAPTER 16
ACCELERATE

Remember Mario, planning that big leadership offsite event?

He was feeling the weight of expectation, initially framing the core challenge around tight budgets and ambitious sales targets, a question that felt heavy, like survival. But then we paused, reframed and landed on something different, which was:

> *'How do we create so much value that customers can't wait to join us and never want to leave, while also achieving profitable growth?'*

That shift wasn't just semantics. It was the spark that ignited a completely different kind of energy, not just for Mario, but eventually for the 180 leaders in that room.

It created a shared moment, an invitation to think about the possibilities, not just pressures. And the result wasn't just a smoother meeting; it was genuine, energised, shared momentum that carried well beyond the offsite itself.

This chapter is about how *you* can deliberately create that same dynamic. More specifically:

- How you can move a group from scattered thinking and colliding assumptions to focused energy and aligned action
- How you can accelerate real progress, together

It starts by consciously creating the container for collective thinking.

CREATING THE SHARED MOMENT

When a group is spinning its wheels, talking past each other or stuck in reactive thinking, the most powerful intervention isn't necessarily a better presentation, more data or a tighter agenda (though those might have their place).

The fundamental intervention is to create a shared Moment, anchored by a shared Critical Question that people genuinely care about.

This isn't just about getting everyone to focus on the same *topic*; it's about finding a question that resonates and taps into a shared sense of purpose or a challenge that feels meaningful *to the group*.

Why is this 'caring' part so important?

Because, as we saw when exploring Questioneering earlier, the right kind of question flips the brain's energy. Instead of triggering defensiveness or the urge to escape discomfort (running away from the situation), a question people care about invites curiosity, engagement and a willingness to explore (leaning into the possibility as well as the challenge). It shifts the underlying motivation from obligation or pressure to contribution and opportunity.

This shared moment, built around a question that matters *to the collective*, acts like a powerful lens, bringing the group's scattered cognitive energy into sharp focus. Consequently, instead of everyone looking at the situation through their own individual filters and assumptions, the shared question invites them to look *at the same thing, at the same time, together*, with a shared desire to figure it out.

It provides the *collective cognitive gravity* needed to counteract the forces of fragmentation we just explored.

But why is this effective?

- **Defining the real work:** A well-crafted shared question clarifies the actual thinking task at hand, moving beyond surface-level challenges or individual priorities.

- **Aligning attention and energy:** It gives everyone a common point to orbit around, reducing the mental energy wasted trying to decipher different agendas and replacing resistance with resonance.

- **Inviting contribution:** A good question doesn't dictate the answer; it opens up space for diverse insights and perspectives towards a common goal people care about.

This deliberate act of establishing a shared Moment, built around a critical, cared-about question, is the essential first step towards unlocking genuine *shared momentum*.

> *Without that resonant starting point, you're likely to stay stuck in the unproductive collision of good intentions.*

THE RIPPLE EFFECT: ENERGY, TRACTION AND ALIGNMENT

When you successfully create that shared Moment, the shift in the room is often palpable. You can literally *feel* it.

I was once leading an event with 50 leaders. The CEO of the organisation walked into the room at the end of the event expecting tired faces and couldn't believe how it was buzzing with enthusiasm? He said he'd never seen so much energy at 3 o'clock on a Friday afternoon.

So, if it wasn't too much caffeine, what was it?

When a group truly enters the same Moment, anchored by a question they care about, three things happen.

- **Energy becomes contagious**

  The cognitive load feels lighter because people aren't carrying the burden of misalignment or internal resistance. Performance anxiety drops and people start contributing more freely. This shared thinking generates its own positive energy, the kind that fuels progress rather than drains reserves.

- **Traction replaces mere activity**

  The group stops just spinning its wheels. Conversations feel like they're actually *going somewhere*. It doesn't have to mean instant agreement, but it feels like the group has gripped the road; there's traction. You're moving together, navigating the challenges with a shared sense of direction.

- **Alignment deepens beyond agreement**

  This is crucial. As I mentioned earlier, agreement is often superficial, a nod to the proposed answer or plan, maybe just to end the discussion. It focuses on closure. Alignment, however, is about the shared understanding *underneath* the answer. It's the shared commitment to the Critical Question and the shared clarity about what matters most in navigating it.

Agreement can be fragile; alignment is resilient.

When a group is truly aligned within the same Moment, they can handle disagreement or unexpected bumps constructively, because their core focus remains shared and meaningful.

And when that deep alignment happens, something fascinating occurs with our Autopilots. Those very patterns that cause collisions when fragmented, start functioning as valuable contributions *for the group*.

- The **Driver's** focus on progress keeps the aligned group moving forward *on the shared quest*.

- The **Fact-Finder's** rigour ensures the shared exploration is well-grounded *and relevant.*

- The **Pioneer's** perspective brings fresh angles *to the shared question everyone cares about.*

- The **Connector's** awareness helps maintain coherence and shared meaning *as the group navigates together.*

- The **Optimiser's** attention to detail helps refine the emerging solution *against the shared criteria of value.*

Guided by the shared Moment and a meaningful Critical Question, these individual thinking patterns transform from *potential liabilities* into *collective assets.*

Diversity of thought becomes a powerful engine for shared momentum, not a source of friction.

Furthermore, this process of thinking together builds something incredibly valuable over time. As a group consistently practices entering shared Moments and navigating challenges with shared focus, they begin to weave that 'Vital Thread' of clarity we touched upon back in Chapter 5. It's the underlying shared logic that crystalises what truly matters and how value is created.

Whether explicitly captured in a framework like The Vital Thread or simply cultivated through consistent practice, it's this deeper alignment that acts as a flexible guide. Unlike a rigid plan that shatters under pressure, this shared thread allows the group to adapt and maintain momentum even when the external landscape shifts dramatically.

It enables truly scalable and adaptive collaboration no matter where people are located. Critically, it ensures that everyone understands not just what is important, but *what makes it* important (or not).

And, in highly disrupted environments where what was true yesterday, may not be today, that depth of clarity is priceless.

MAKE IT REAL

Reflect on what's been covered in this chapter so far.

How has what has been described shown up in your own experience?

_____

_____

_____

Can you think of a time, in a group setting, where you have felt a sense of momentum? What did it feel like?

_____

_____

_____

How did that impact the speed and quality of the work that needed to be done?

_____

_____

_____

Key takeaway:

In a human setting, momentum and inertia are easier to feel than see. So, next time you are in a group, pay attention to the energy in the room. Is it high or low? Is it positive or negative? Noticing this in everyday situations will enable you to know when you're Accelerating effectively.

ACCELERATING BY DESIGN

Okay, so creating shared Moments around Critical Questions that people care about ignites shared momentum.

But how do you actually *do* it?

It requires conscious design and Questioneering confidence. Remember, you're essentially applying the first three levels of mastery: Activate, Articulate and Navigate, at scale, with multiple brains, in real time.

This takes skill and it's why Accelerate sits at Level 4 in The Moment Method. Once you reach this level, there are some key principles to keep in mind.

Get the right people involved

Who needs to be part of this thinking? It's not always just the most senior people or those who are physically nearest. Consider who holds relevant insight, diverse perspectives, key influence (formal or informal) and who will be crucial for carrying the momentum forward.

Sometimes, starting with a smaller core group and using a *snowball approach*, where that initial group gains clarity and then invites the next layer into the thinking. Then, once the combined group has clarity, they invite another layer of people.

This approach can be very effective for building ownership organically.

Always start with 'sensemaking'

Jumping into solutions before understanding the group's collective starting point inevitably leads to focusing on the wrong content. Don't rush to action. First, create space to map where people are, mentally and emotionally.

- What different perspectives, tensions or assumptions are present in the room?
- What does each person think this Moment is really about?

If you don't collectively orient to the cognitive landscape first, any map you draw will likely lead you astray.

Questions like: *'What's the real moment we find ourselves in together right now?'* or *'Before we dive deeper, what's the most vital question we need to ask as a group?'* aren't just warm-ups; they are crucial interventions to establish a shared foundation for meaningful thinking.

Make the thinking visible

Shared physical artefacts get the core question, key insights, emerging tensions and potential pathways out of people's heads and onto something everyone can see. You can use more traditional tools like whiteboards, flip charts, a virtual collaboration board or shared notes. Or, get a bit more creative.

In my experience, anything that you can physically hold, can usually serve as a visualisation tool. It just takes a little imagination.

This approach ensures insights become tangible contributions, not just fleeting comments. Visibility also allows people to connect dots, build on each other's thinking and track the collective journey. It turns individual thoughts into shared assets and helps clarity compound.

Give every question a clear intention

Purposeful questions guide cognitive energy effectively, while vague ones dissipate it. If you're leading the conversation, be clear *why* you're asking a particular question *at this point*.

What are you trying to achieve with this question? Are you trying to:

- surface hidden assumptions (Exploring)?
- identify root causes and options (Solving)?
- gather specific information (Learning)?
- generate next steps (Doing)?
- check for shared understanding (Sensemaking)?

If the intention isn't clear, the question might confuse rather than clarify. Or, worse, it might cause people to disengage. You're not just managing a discussion; you're consciously guiding the group's thinking energy toward a productive outcome.

The rock-climbing metaphor is, once again, useful here.

Asking the wrong question is like offering a foot hold that is too far away to physically reach. Both create risk and when our brain senses it, people stop focusing on the shared Moment and retreat to default thinking.

Watch out for quasi-questions

Be mindful of questions that aren't really questions at all, but rather opinions, judgments or attempts to steer the outcome disguised as inquiry (eg. *'Don't you think we should just focus on X?'*).

Quasi-questions shut down genuine inquiry and signal that the goal is compliance, not co-creation. They also undermine psychological safety. They're less about genuine discovery and more about steering toward a conclusion *the asker* already has in mind.

And people can feel it. That's when they start playing safe, deferring to the speaker, or mentally and emotionally 'checking out' entirely.

---

*Remember, the goal isn't to funnel the group towards **your answer**; it's to hold the space for the best answer to emerge from the collective thinking.*

It's not about cleverly engineering agreement. It's about authentically creating a Moment and framing a question that people *want* to engage with, because it feels real, important and open to genuine contribution.

When you do that, the ownership becomes genuine, the momentum becomes sustainable, and you collectively stay out of The Answer Trap while achieving far better outcomes.

But, what does that look like when it works?

UNLOCKING MOMENTUM: EMMA'S STORY

If you truly want to accelerate progress and escape The Answer Trap as a group, you have to be willing to let go of the answer *you* walked in with, even if (especially if!) it feels comfortable and right to you.

The magic of shared thinking is that it can take you somewhere better, somewhere richer, somewhere you couldn't have envisioned on your own.

That's not a loss of control; it's sophisticated and it's the essential of modern leadership in complexity.

My client Emma offers a great example.

As Director of Infrastructure Projects in a government department, her team of 80 skilled professionals were feeling the pressure: capability gaps, internal resistance and the weight of delivering a transformation they hadn't fully shaped together.

Emma's initial instinct might have been to push harder on the strategy's execution. But our early conversations revealed the core issue wasn't just commitment; it was disconnection. People felt removed from the central thinking, caught in reactive patterns, trying to deliver complex work without a shared 'why' or 'how'. They were collectively stuck.

What Emma needed wasn't just a clearer message; she needed a truly shared Moment.

We started by creating dedicated thinking space for her leadership team. Instead of immediately problem-solving, we focused on Articulating The Moment with a Critical Question that revealed the underlying dynamics. It looked something like this.

- *'What are the thinking patterns and assumptions currently keeping us stuck and how could we shift our approach to move forward effectively together?'*

That single, focused session shifted the dynamic. The pace slowed intentionally, defensiveness eased and real issues surfaced. The team used The Moment Method not just as a concept, but as a tool to diagnose their own patterns. They moved from feeling constrained by the situation to taking ownership of how they responded to it.

Then, crucially, we scaled it.

In a single one-day event with 80 people in the room, the leadership team facilitated similar conversations with each other's team and peers, using the same core questions and thinking structures. They didn't just cascade decisions; they propagated the *thinking process*. They created a chain reaction of shared Moments.

The impact was both sustained and significant. 10 months later, the internal People Matters survey told the story.

- Motivation ('My organisation motivates me to help it achieve its objectives') soared from 67% the previous year to 85%.

- Inspiration ('My organisation inspires me to do my best work') jumped from 67% to 79%.

These weren't fleeting boosts. Emma confirmed that our work together had led to this sustained shift. And, that the results were a direct result of The Moment Method fostering genuine alignment, clarity and co-ownership across the division.

People didn't just understand the strategy anymore; they felt *part* of shaping and driving it.

This is the kind of outcome possible when you get Accelerate right. And, thanks to the power of questions and Questioneering, Mastery Level 4 enables the whole group to make greater progress, faster.

FROM SHARED MOMENTUM TO SUSTAINED CULTURE

Accelerate, is how we take the individual capacity to navigate complexity and scale it to the collective. It's powerful and energising.

But creating powerful moments isn't quite the end of the story.

- How do we ensure this way of thinking isn't just a flash in the pan during an offsite or a specific project?

- How does it move from being a deliberate intervention to becoming just the way we naturally operate?

- How does it seep into the fabric of everyday interactions?

That's the final stage of our journey with The Moment Method. Because the ultimate goal isn't just to accelerate progress in a singular Moment that matters right now. It's to build an environment, a team, an organisation, maybe just an everyday conversational rhythm, where this kind of thoughtful, deliberate, shared thinking becomes the norm.

A readily accessible way for any number of people to think and work together, especially when things get disrupted.

And that transition, from accelerating a moment to fostering a culture, is where we head next. It's the fifth and final level of mastery in the Moment Method: **Cultivate**.

CHAPTER IN A NUTSHELL

- Shared momentum doesn't happen by accident - it's created by designing moments that matter, together.

- When groups get stuck, the solution isn't more data or better plans - it's a shared Critical Question people care about.

- A shared moment brings scattered thinking into focus, transforming friction into traction and alignment into action.

- Autopilots stop colliding and start contributing when guided by a meaningful, collective question.

- Deliberately designing for acceleration means making thinking visible, engaging the right mix of people and asking purposeful questions.

- When done well, Accelerate turns a group's diversity into momentum - and builds ownership that lasts well beyond The Moment.

CHAPTER 17
CULTIVATE

Sometimes, the most profound shifts happen in the most ordinary settings?

It was dinner time at Tom's house. Midweek rush, everyone a bit frazzled. Tom, who coaches a local youth soccer team, slumped into his chair, the weight of the world seemingly on his shoulders. You could feel the frustration before he even spoke.

'They're just not getting it,' he sighed, poking at his pasta. 'The semi-finals are only three weeks away and we're still missing basic transitions. I've explained it, walked them through it, drawn the plays on the whiteboard. Over and over.'

His partner looked up, 'What's the specific bit that's not landing?'

'The movement *after* we win possession,' Tom explained. 'They just freeze for a split second. They don't instinctively move into space to receive the next pass.

I keep telling them, if they just *do* what we practised, anticipate, step into space, trust the run, the whole attacking play opens up. But they hesitate. It's like they're waiting to be explicitly told exactly where to go every single time.'

There was a brief pause around the table. Then Tom's 10-year-old daughter, mid-chew on some garlic bread, looked up with genuine curiosity and asked:

'Dad, do they know *why* it matters?'

Tom frowned slightly. 'What do you mean 'why it matters'?'

She shrugged, matter-of-factly. 'Like… do they actually get *how* moving into space right away helps *win the game*?'

That simple question stopped him cold. He'd been relentlessly focused on the *mechanics*, the steps, the drills, the 'what' and the 'how'. But his daughter, in her innocent wisdom, had gone straight to the missing piece: the *purpose*, the 'why'.

The next day at training, Tom changed his approach.

He didn't introduce a complex new drill. He started with a different kind of question, gathering the players around.

'Hey team, quick question. When we win the ball back from them, right in that instant, what's the absolute *best thing* that could possibly happen next for us?'

The players paused. Thought. A few hesitant hands went up, then more confidently.

One player offered, 'Well, *we* have the momentum then… we could launch a surprise attack before they regroup.'

Another added, 'Yeah, we could catch their defence out of position if we move fast.'

Suddenly, they weren't just hearing instructions; they were seeing the *opportunity*. They started connecting the tactical instruction (move into space) with the strategic outcome (scoring goals, winning the game). They grasped the 'why'.

And when they started scrimmaging, the change was noticeable. Not perfect, but visible. The hesitation started to decrease. The movement into space became more instinctive.

Not because of a better drill. Because of a better question, one that connected the action to the purpose.

This is the essence of Cultivation: nurturing a culture that thinks together, especially in turbulent times.

WHY CULTIVATION MATTERS

There is a reason that Cultivate sits at Level 5 in The Moment Method. Even when we *know* how to think well, have *personally experienced* the energy and clarity that comes from escaping The Answer Trap and creating shared moments, the surrounding environment often exerts a powerful gravitational pull back towards the old, familiar ways.

Back towards:

- certainty over curiosity.

- control over collaboration.

- speed over depth.

- the safety of easy answers over the discomfort of exploration.

This pull isn't necessarily malicious. It's simply how many of our systems, workplaces and social expectations are implicitly wired.

So, even after a really successful Accelerate session where everyone felt the power of shared thinking, the default pressures of deadlines, targets, expectations and ingrained habits can quickly pull individuals and groups right back into reactive Autopilot modes.

That cultural pull is strong, persistent and requires conscious, ongoing effort to resist.

And *that's* why this final level of mastery, Cultivate, is so essential.

Thinking well isn't just a skill to be learnt in isolation; it's a practice that needs to be *valued, nurtured, protected* and *embedded* until it becomes a resilient part of the *culture.*

---

*Culture isn't just the way we do things around here.
It's also the way we do thinking around here. It's not
what we think, it's how we think.*

A culture doesn't sustain itself by accident, especially when it involves swimming slightly against the current of conventional expectations.

If we want to protect and grow this capacity for better thinking, we have to actively Cultivate it. One conversation, one meeting, one question and one Moment at a time.

THE FRICTION OF REALITY

Let's be really honest here.

Even if you're completely sold on the value of The Moment Method and you've seen first-hand what a powerful question can do, there's probably still that little voice of hesitation that pipes up sometimes. This can be especially so when the pressure is on or you're not the most senior person in the room. It might sound like:

- 'Is it really my place to slow things down?'
- 'What if I ask something that sounds naive or derails the agenda?'
- 'People expect me to be decisive right now, not questioning.'
- 'This feels a bit risky...'

That voice isn't just resistance; it reflects the genuine reality of many environments.

We operate in cultures that often implicitly value speed, clarity and control. We've likely all been rewarded at some point for having a quick answer, sounding certain or keeping things moving smoothly.

So, that hesitation we feel when we consider pausing, asking a real, open question, one you don't already know the answer to, *can* feel like stepping out on a limb. It signals uncertainty in contexts that might prefer confidence and opens up space when the pressure might be demanding closure.

Women in leadership roles, especially in traditionally male-dominated industries, can find this pressure particularly strong. They want to prove they are just as smart and competent as their male colleagues. And, asking questions rather than giving confident answers can feel vulnerable, even self-sabotaging.

But there's a counter-intuitive truth that I've learnt through my own leadership and from working with countless leaders and teams.

People rarely need you to have all the answers. What they often desperately need, especially in complex situations, is for someone to help them think more clearly, together.

And that kind of collaborative thinking often doesn't even *begin* until someone has the courage to gently interrupt the premature rush to clarity, the default assumptions and the easy answers.

MAKE IT REAL

Think about a group of which you are a member. It can be at work or in life.

How would you describe its culture, within the context of what we've discussed in this chapter?

What role do you play in it maintaining or changing that culture?

What role would you like to play?

What stops you?

Key takeaway:

Cultivation doesn't mean that you need to be relentlessly bold or confrontational. It's much quieter and more consistent than that. It's about noticing The Moments where thinking gets stuck, shallow or fragmented and choosing to treat those moments with care, offering a small nudge towards deeper engagement. It starts with how *you* show up.

SHAPE THE CULTURE BY SHAPING THE MOMENT

Cultivating an environment for better thinking isn't about launching a grand initiative. It concerns the small, consistent choices you make in everyday interactions. It's subtly shifting the dynamics, one moment at a time.

But how can you do that? Here are a few ways to get started.

Model the pause, own the question

The most powerful way to influence culture is through your own actions. Don't just talk about The Moment Method; embody its principles, especially when others can observe you.

- **Consciously pause before reacting**, even for just a breath.

- **Verbalise your own thinking process occasionally:** 'The question I'm wrestling with right now is...' or 'I'm noticing I have an urge to jump to a solution here, but I wonder if we need to explore X first.'

- **Acknowledge uncertainty openly and calmly:** 'That's a great point, I actually don't know the answer yet, let me think about that,' or 'This next step is too important for us to just react. Let's make sure we get is right.'

- **Resist the impulse** to immediately fill silences after asking a thoughtful question; allow space for others to think.

When people see you modelling thoughtful engagement, owning your questions and comfortably sitting with uncertainty instead of projecting false certainty, it creates implicit permission and safety for them to do the same.

Wield signature questions wisely

By now, you have a sense of your own Autopilot pattern and perhaps those of people you spend time with regularly. Remember, these patterns aren't just liabilities; they hold cognitive strengths.

Cultivation involves consciously shifting from reactive Autopilot to intentional Copilot, using these strengths as contributions. A simple way to do this is by deploying what I call a 'signature question'.

A signature question is your Autopilots default question but reframed in an intentional and positive way. There are two ways to use it.

Offer your own signature question

Instead of reacting from your default (eg. a Driver pushing *any* action), consciously offer the more constructive Copilot version (*'What would meaningful progress actually look like right now?'*).

Frame your contribution around the *strength* of your pattern (eg. 'My Driver brain wants to get moving, so maybe the helpful question now is, what does real progress look like?').

Invite others' signature questions

Recognise when the group might benefit from a different thinking style.

Instead of getting frustrated ('Why is he always focused on risk?'), invite that perspective constructively: 'That's an interesting angle. From your perspective what's the key risk we need to be mindful of as we explore this possibility [Optimiser]?' or 'To make sure we're grounded, what do we already reliably know about this situation [Fact-Finder]?'

Using Signature Questions intentionally helps transform potential points of friction into valuable, diverse inputs, building a richer collective understanding.

Invite thinking, don't demand it

As we've already talked about, asking questions can feel risky. How you introduce your question matters enormously in creating an environment where people feel safe enough to think openly rather than defensively. You're not just posing a query; you're issuing an invitation into a potentially different kind of conversation.

- **Use curiosity starters:**

    'I'm just curious about...' or 'Help me understand...' or 'Could we explore X for a moment?'

- **Soften the entry:**

    'This might be slightly off-piste, but I'm wondering...' or 'Just playing devil's advocate here...' or 'No final answer needed, but what if...?'

- **Emphasise shared exploration:**

    'How might we look at this from this angle?' or 'I wonder if we're all seeing this the same way.'

These kinds of frames signal care, lower the perceived stakes and make it easier for people to engage with the question rather than reacting to the perceived challenge.

Your aim is to open the door to thinking, not force people through it. What you're doing is inviting others to join you in a Moment that they may not yet have noticed.

Go for the triple jump, not just the long jump

It's tempting to ask a big question because if you can get that answer, you'll feel like you'll move forward faster. However, a big question asked too soon can leave people's brains behind. You can quickly find that the only person listening... is you.

You don't always need a perfectly crafted, profound question to Cultivate better thinking. Sometimes, the most effective approach is a series of small, gentle nudges that subtly disrupt a reactive or stuck pattern. Think in triples.

HOP Observe/Pause	SKIP Clarify/Focus	JUMP Invite Exploration
'How do this conversation is going so far?'	'What was the original question we started with?'	'What's one assumption we're making that might be worth testing?'

These micro-moves, delivered calmly, can gently shift the group's energy and thinking rhythm without feeling like a major intervention.

Avoid killer questions

Just as important as knowing how to invite thinking is recognising the kinds of questions that reliably kill it. Be mindful to avoid questions that, intentionally or not, trigger defensiveness, blame or compliance:

- **Accusatory questions** (*'Why didn't you...?'*) create blame, not insight.

- **Interrogations** (*'Have you even thought this through?'*) feel like attacks.

- **Rapid-fire fixes** (*'So what's the answer then?'*) shut down exploration prematurely.

- **Show-off questions** (overly complex or jargon-filled) prioritise the asker's ego over collective understanding.

Cultivating better thinking requires asking questions designed to genuinely open up space, not implicitly close it down.

THE TIPPING POINT

There's a fascinating transition that can happen when these Cultivation practices become more frequent and widespread within a group or organisation. Initially, it requires conscious effort from individuals like you – modelling the behaviour, asking the framing questions and creating the space.

But over time, if the practice is consistent, the questions asked prove genuinely useful and if people experience the positive energy of real shared thinking, something starts to shift more deeply.

The practices become internalised. People start pausing themselves more often and begin reframing questions more instinctively. They naturally start inviting others into The Moment, using Questioneering as a day-to-day skill.

And when enough people adopt these behaviours consistently and naturally, a powerful transformation happens: the system starts thinking for itself.

The capacity for navigating complexity becomes embedded in the group's norms and reflexes, not just reliant on specific individuals remembering to 'use the method'. It becomes less of an intervention and more of 'the way we do things around here when it gets tricky'.

So, how does this play out in reality?

THE PRACTICAL POWER OF MASTERING THE MOMENT

Let's step inside a real example of what this looks like when it works – not just as a one-off intervention, but as a sustained cultural shift. What follows, shows how a team facing real complexity found a new rhythm for thinking – together.

One of my clients, Mark, was the General Manager for Decommissioned Infrastructure at a global renewables company. He oversaw 20 retired renewable energy sites across the UK and Europe – wind farms, solar fields and hydro stations that were no longer active but still required long-term environmental, regulatory and strategic oversight.

It's high-stakes work that blends science, regulation, politics and economics. And for a long time, Mark's team was stuck. Not because they weren't capable, but because the problems they were facing didn't respond well to the usual tools. They were being asked to 'solve the decommissioning problem', but no matter how hard they pushed, progress felt just out of reach.

Mark first came across The Moment Method when I was being interviewed on a podcast, talking about Questioneering and how to lead our thinking in complexity. Something clicked. He told me later it was like someone had put words to the frustration he couldn't quite name. He realised their team wasn't failing – they were working in a way that made breakthroughs nearly impossible.

Shifting the frame

That's when we started working together. And instead of launching another plan or ramping up execution, we did something different. We paused, stepped back and reframed the situation. Then, we introduced the idea of treating the way they were thinking (not what they were doing) as the primary focus.

That alone began to shift the energy.

Engineers who were used to solving tangible, practical problems started making space for ambiguity. Legal and environmental teams, who often clashed over competing priorities, began seeing challenges through each other's eyes. One practice that stuck was the idea of 'seeing the dark side of the mountain' (a shorthand from The Moment Method) used to remind themselves to consider perspectives that weren't immediately visible from their own vantage point.

This wasn't a one-off training. It was real thinking, learnt in real time by applying it to real Moments that mattered.

From insight to rhythm

One of the early turning points came when a member of the senior leadership team unexpectedly left. There was pressure to act quickly – to redistribute tasks, fill the gap, make quick decisions. But instead of rushing in, the team paused and Activated The Moment.

They sat down together and used structured Questioneering to unpack what was really needed. In just 30 minutes, they moved from scattered stress to shared clarity. Not because they had a perfect answer, but because they had the *space, structure and strategies* to move forward with confidence.

That experience stuck. From then on, they began running monthly Moment Method sessions. They picked a real Moment and spent one hour, collectively Activating, Articulating and Navigating it. It was something they kept returning to.

Over time, the ripple effects grew.

Other teams started borrowing the language. Executives noticed the shift. Collaboration improved. There was less rushing to premature answers and more curiosity, more energy and more momentum.

A system starting to think for itself

At first, Mark's boss was a little sceptical. But gradually, even he began to see the difference. Frustration dropped. Engagement lifted. Decisions became more thoughtful and more durable. The language of questions, of pause, of shared exploration started showing up in meetings without prompting.

That's when you know culture is shifting. Mark and his team weren't just applying The Moment Method. They were living it.

And they kept practising, long after our formal work had ended. Not only because it worked, but because it made hard work feel meaningful again.

I caught up with Mark a year later. His leaders were now teaching new employees the role Questioneering played in their culture. Mark captured the power of Cultivation beautifully:

'A lot of organisations will say, go faster, fix this, fix this, fix this! But at the end of the day, if you're left saying 'Well, I've got this thing. And I can't bash it with a hammer anymore', then it's time to find a different approach'

'It's a lot more words than we engineers are used to but… it also makes the conversation a lot more fun'.

FROM THINKING WELL TO THINKING TOGETHER

So, that's *Cultivate* - the fifth and final Mastery Level in the Moment Method.

If you've come this far - if you've tested what it means to Activate, Articulate, Navigate, Accelerate and now Cultivate - you've done more than just read about a method. You've likely begun to rewire some deeply embedded habits in your own thinking.

My hope is that by now, you're beginning to experience the ripple effect. You're realising that how you show up - how you pause, reframe or invite others into The Moment - can shift the dynamic around you.

That's the promise of Cultivate. It reminds us that escaping The Answer Trap isn't just about mastering your own Moments. It's about creating environments where others are less likely to fall into it in the first place.

And you don't need formal authority to do that.

- Every moment *you* choose to pause instead of reacting.
- Every time *you* gently reframe a problem into a possibility.
- Every question *you* ask that helps others see the 'why' or consider a different angle.
- Every instance *you* create space for a quieter voice or a less conventional idea.

Each offers a chance to shape how thinking happens - not in grand, dramatic ways, but in small, consistent, meaningful ones. That's how systems change. Not through mandates, slogans or posters, but through lived experience.

One team discovers something that helps.

They share it.

Others try it.

Momentum builds.

And then… the culture begins to shift.

***

MAKE CLARITY CONTAGIOUS

When we started Part 4, we asked: how do you take the clarity you've created for yourself and help it ripple outwards?

Now you've seen what that really takes. Not just better tools or smarter individuals - but shared Moments. The kind that create traction, not just activity. Ownership, not just compliance. And thinking that strengthens under pressure, rather than fragmenting.

You've also seen what gets in the way: Colliding Autopilots, misaligned Moments and the pressure to perform rather than pause. And you've seen how - through Activate, Articulate, Navigate, Accelerate and Cultivate - you can build the habits, language and rhythms that counteract those forces.

In this part of the book, we've explored how clarity scales when it's nurtured. Momentum becomes collective when it's created on purpose. And better thinking becomes culture when it's practised in The Moments that matter.

This isn't just a leadership skill. It's a human capability. And it's one we need to protect and grow - not just for ourselves, but for what's coming next.

In the final chapter, we'll step back one last time. Not to introduce another concept - but to reflect on the bigger picture.

- What's really at stake when we stay trapped in reactive think-ing? And what becomes possible when we don't?

Let's go there together.

CHAPTER IN A NUTSHELL

- Better thinking won't stick unless we deliberately nurture it - it needs to be cultivated until it becomes how we work, not just what we know.

- Cultural gravity pulls us back toward speed, certainty and control; Cultivate helps us hold the line and grow a different norm.

- You don't need authority to lead this shift - every moment you pause, reframe or ask a better question can shape the system around you.

- Small, consistent moves - modelling your Copilot, using signature questions, creating safety and shifting the energy - build collective clarity.

- When enough people practice this deliberately, the system begins to think for itself. The method stops being something you use and becomes the way you lead, decide and collaborate.

- Cultivate isn't about changing culture overnight - it's about changing the next conversation on purpose and letting that ripple outwards.

PART 5

THE HUMAN IMPERATIVE

CHAPTER 18

YOUR MIND.
YOUR MOMENT.

I asked AI to help me write a book.

What it gave back was fast, polished and structured. On the surface, it felt like progress, like I'd found a shortcut around the hardest parts of the work. But sitting with it, a quiet discomfort began to stir. Something vital was missing – the thinking, the wrestle, that moment. It was the unease of realising I'd outsourced not just the typing but the deeper cognitive effort.

This realisation was where our journey together really began.

The problem wasn't the tool itself. It was me. More specifically, it was my brain doing exactly what every human brain is wired to do when faced with ambiguity or the pressure to perform: craving clarity, instinctively avoiding discomfort, reaching for whatever feels like forward movement, even if it's an illusion.

It's a deep, often invisible craving. And now it has a name: **The Answer Trap.**

If you've travelled this far through these pages, you've seen how easily it pulls us in, often without us even noticing.

But now? You can see it everywhere. And, you have 'Your map out of the trap' to help you continue from here.

When you first saw it, the twelve moves through the map may not have been obvious. Now, however, there is greater depth behind each one.

So why not take another look?

- Which of the twelve moves are now clear?
- Which ones are you currently applying?
- Which ones would you like to focus on next?
- Which ones would you like to understand better?

You can continue to come back to these questions as you evolve your insights and capabilities.

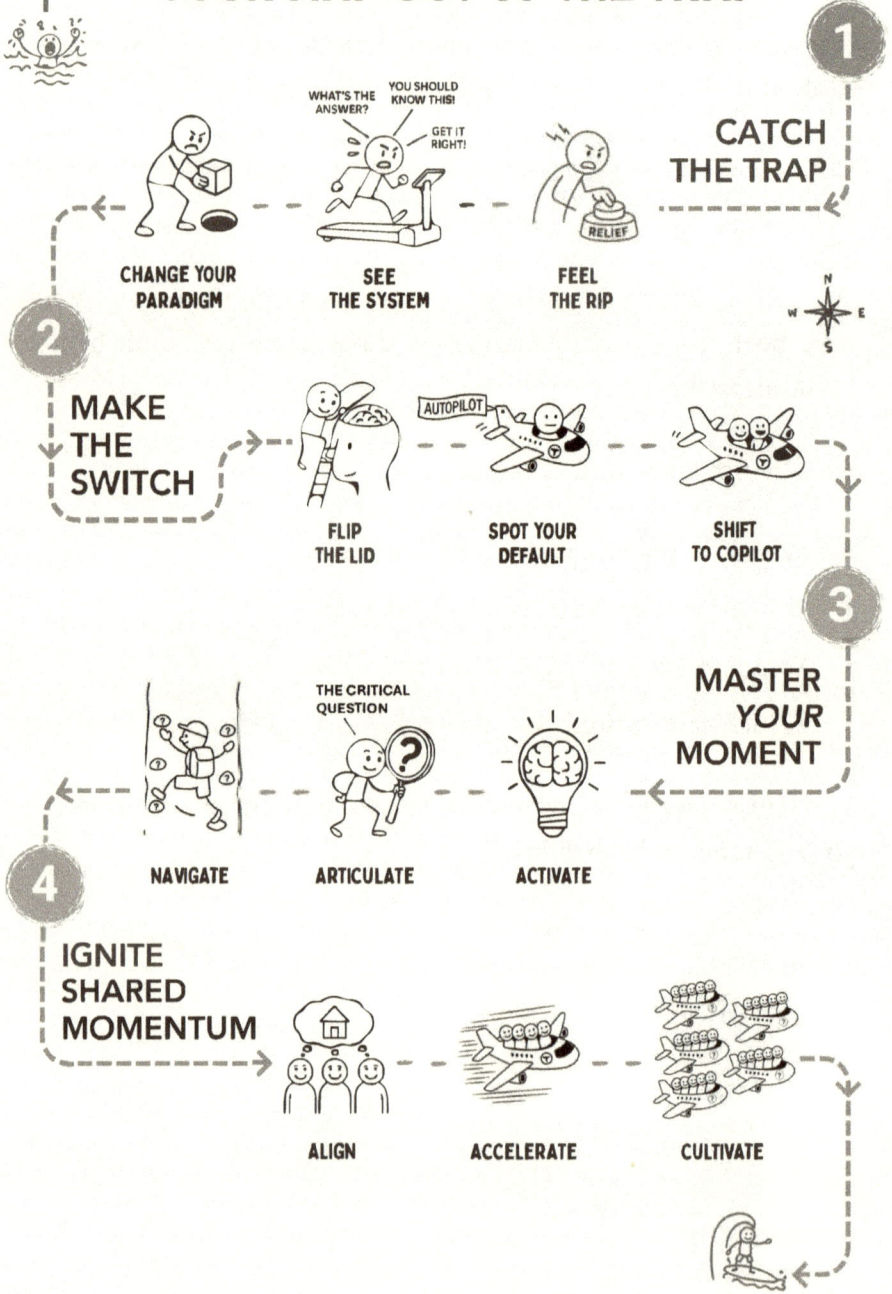

YOUR MAP OUT OF THE TRAP

1

CATCH THE TRAP

CHANGE YOUR PARADIGM

SEE THE SYSTEM

FEEL THE RIP

2

MAKE THE SWITCH

FLIP THE LID

SPOT YOUR DEFAULT

SHIFT TO COPILOT

3

MASTER *YOUR* MOMENT

NAVIGATE

ARTICULATE

ACTIVATE

4

IGNITE SHARED MOMENTUM

ALIGN

ACCELERATE

CULTIVATE

BEYOND THE TRAP: RECLAIMING YOUR THINKING

You've learnt how your brain's protective reflex shows up through your Autopilot. But crucially, you've also learnt how to interrupt that pattern. Also, you now have the five levels of mastery and The Moment Method to help you stay with, and move through, complex, ambiguous situations. This proven approach not only gives your brain the space, structure and strategies it needs. It's also the secret to embracing a new paradigm where we move from merely dealing with disruption, to actively shaping and harnessing the opportunity within it.

Let's face it. That's a lot. And yet, there's more.

Because beneath the methods, the stories and the models, this book has been about something deeper. That is, reclaiming something precious that we are collectively at risk of losing, almost without noticing.

Namely, our ability to think on purpose.

It's our capacity to stay present with uncertainty and to have the agency to choose our response, even – especially – when The Moment itself seems to want to choose for us.

And so, we arrive inevitably at the questions sitting quietly beneath every chapter.

In an age of increasingly intelligent machines and instantly available answers, what kind of human will you decide to be? And what kind of thinking will you choose?

The future is arriving faster than we often realise. The technologies offering shortcuts and certainty are powerful, seductive even. But the real power, the enduring power, still resides in how we choose to engage our own minds.

THE NINE TRUTHS OF THINKING IN THE AGE OF ANSWERS

We've talked a lot about agency. As you've travelled through The Answer Trap, you've uncovered your capacity for conscious choice. Now, as you take these insights forward into the real work – the ongoing practice of meeting each Moment, refining your thinking, wrestling with what's complex – there are nine fundamental truths to anchor you. These aren't just concepts; they are the principles and key messages that will carry you forward.

#1 - The danger isn't AI, it's that we stop thinking for ourselves

When I first tried to outsource this book's writing to AI, I gained speed but lost the essential 'wrestle' of thinking. This turning point revealed the real risk: not AI surpassing us, but our subtle surrender of hard cognitive effort. The Answer Trap quietly lures us to accept surface clarity and skip crucial questions, making us forget when we've stopped thinking for ourselves. AI didn't take away my ability to think; it simply offered an easy way to avoid it.

#2 - The Answer Trap is a survival strategy, not a flaw

Don't judge yourself for falling into The Answer Trap. It's not a flaw, but your brain's protective survival strategy. When faced with uncertainty, your brain instinctively seeks quick clarity and relief, making avoidance feel like progress. This sneakiness gives us something to hold onto when everything else feels shaky. Recognising this natural wiring, not judging it, is what puts you back in control.

#3 - In complexity, thinking is the real work

Thinking isn't just pre-work to be rushed through; it *is* the core contribution. When scenarios shift and answers aren't obvious, the deliberate process of staying with your thinking is the real work. Choosing to keep thinking under pressure isn't just effortful, it's leadership that honours The Moment and prevents costly missteps.

#4 - You can't think your way out by doing more

Like a rip current, trying harder doesn't get you out of The Answer Trap. In complexity, the natural instinct to 'do more' can just make things noisier or bury you deeper. The real shift isn't about effort, but orientation. What's needed is better thinking. A pause to step back, reframe then deliberately choose your approach before speed takes you further off course.

#5 - The disrupted brain tries to feel better, not think better

When disruption hits, your brain quickly chases whatever feels immediately fixable, masking the real issue. Noticing this powerful pull to reduce discomfort is a critical skill. It allows you to catch The Moment and ask what it's *really* asking of you, not just what you can fix fastest.

#6 - You can't navigate complexity on Autopilot

Autopilot is efficient for routine, but it's a liability in complexity. It reacts from habit and can't shift when rules change. Copilot is the conscious part of you that notices this default, presses pause, and insists on choosing how you think, not just reacting. In complexity, that deliberate choice is everything. Most importantly, it's how you take back the wheel.

#7 - Questions are your stepping-stones through the unknown

In complexity, progress isn't just about outputs; it's a shift in your thinking. Questions are the stepping-stones that make this possible. They keep thinking alive, re-engage your brain, and reframe The Moment, driving real momentum even if final answers haven't landed yet. If your thinking has evolved, that is progress.

#8 - We break free together (or not at all)

The Answer Trap is contagious; groups can quickly mirror urgency and reward untested certainty, even if individuals are capable. Escaping it isn't just individual awareness, but about what we model and invite from others. Shared clarity in complexity doesn't emerge from individual brilliance, but from collective thinking and creating just enough space for others to think differently.

#9 - This isn't just a toolkit, it's a human imperative

This book offers practical tools. However, its deeper message is about staying human, intentional, and protecting the depth and care complex problems require, because no tool or AI can do that thinking for us. This work isn't optional; it's how we stay capable and clear in a fast-changing world, meeting The Moment with presence and responsibility, because questions now matter more than ever.

THE THREE PLAYERS IN EVERY CHOICE

Almost every decision you make today is shaped by three players, even if you're not always aware of them.

There's **you** – the conscious human, capable of reflection, guided by values, holding agency and the power to choose. There's **your brain** – a fast, efficient biological machine, wired for pattern recognition and survival.

And there's the **digital brain** – the ever-present web of algorithms, systems and AI, operating at speed, offering answers and nudging your thinking in subtle ways.

This third player isn't just generative AI. It's already embedded in your everyday life. It's the GPS that removes your need to think spatially. The calendar that arranges your week before you've decided what matters. The search engine that finishes your sentence and sometimes even chooses the question. These tools are helpful, no doubt. But every time they remove friction, they also remove a small moment of conscious thought. And over time, those moments matter.

We're not thinking in isolation anymore. In fact, we haven't been for a while. Importantly, your role is not to reject either the biological brain or the digital one. It's to learn how to lead both.

Your biological brain is brilliant in its own way. It reacts instantly when it senses threat. It protects you, adapts quickly and knows how to conserve energy. But it's also reactive and doesn't naturally pause when uncertainty spikes. It just wants the discomfort to stop.

The digital brain is equally impressive in its domain.

It processes more information than we can imagine and offers fluent, fast responses that sound confident and complete. But it doesn't understand what matters or hold values. It can't discern context or feel responsible for outcomes. It offers options; it just doesn't care which one you choose.

That leaves **you**.

The only one who can pause. The only one who can feel the tension in a room, notice The Moment your thinking starts to narrow and ask, 'What kind of thinking is really needed here?'

That pause is what puts you back in control. It's not about being perfect or always making the right decision. It's means noticing when you're being pulled by instinct or nudged by a system – and choosing to think anyway.

In disruption, that's the real work. Not resisting technology. Not blaming your biology. But stepping into The Moment between stimulus and response and leading both.

OUR HUMAN EDGE

This act of stepping into The Moment, of learning to lead both biological and digital influences, reveals our essential human edge. AI can respond faster than any of us. It can summarise a decade's worth of research in seconds, mimic tone and generate plausible next steps without breaking into a sweat.

That's not science fiction anymore; it's daily reality. But speed and fluency aren't the whole picture.

The real power of human thinking has never been about doing things faster (although some of us might like to think this was the case). It's been about knowing when to slow down.

When to ask a better question or to pay attention to something that doesn't quite fit. And, when to stop and sense what might be going unsaid.

AI can't do that. But *you* can.

That's the edge we carry forward. Not because we're perfect thinkers, but because we're capable of choosing how we think. Our strength isn't in out-performing machines. It's in doing the thing they can't: staying human in The Moments that matter most.

These days, being smart is no longer about having all the answers or being the fastest. Now, with endless information and AI at our fingertips, your true advantage lies in your ability to weigh not just what's possible or logical, but what's *meaningful, useful, ethical* or *desirable.*

To **sense** when a situation needs **care**, not just completion. To **ask**, 'Does this really matter? Is this the decision we want to stand behind?', especially when the answer looks tidy but something still feels off.

That's the edge we carry forward.

THIS IS OUR MOMENT

The real work, the ongoing practice, begins now.

It's not the kind of work you schedule neatly into your calendar or capture perfectly on a whiteboard. The real work happens in the countless micro-moments you might previously have barely noticed.

The ones where you now catch yourself defaulting to speed over reflection. Or, in which you feel that familiar pull to appear as though you have all the answers, instead of acknowledging that some things remain unclear. Also, in those times when you sense the discomfort of uncertainty rising and feel the almost over-whelming urge to close it off, quickly.

You don't need a manifesto pinned above your desk or anyone else's permission. You just need to develop the habit of noticing the next Moment as it arises – and choosing to think deliberately and help others do the same.

You now have a method. A way to return what The Answer Trap takes away: space, structure and strategy. You've started to flex your mental muscles.

Now, it's up to you to cultivate the rhythm, one conscious choice at a time. You won't always get it right. You'll still fall into The Answer Trap sometimes; we all do.

But the difference now is that you can recognise the pull. You know how to re-enter The Moment, even if you've already started to slide. And, you also have the tools and techniques to lead your thinking and perhaps, gently guide others, from the inside out.

You don't have to fix the whole system. You just need to recognise when the next Moment comes along and decide to do something different. That's enough.

Ultimately, when we distil everything down to what really matters, the greatest risk isn't that AI will replace us. It's that we'll collectively forget what it truly means to be human – and to think.

This is our Moment. The window is still open. We still get to choose.

Will we evolve our thinking, consciously and deliberately? Or will we surrender it, quietly and without noticing?

The choice is ours. Let's make it wisely.

AN INVITATION

Dear Reader,

We've reached the end of the book, but it doesn't have to stop here. If its content has resonated and you want to:

- take your thinking and capability to the next level
- access practical strategies to navigate a culture that rewards quick answers over real clarity
- be part of a bigger conversation about breaking free in a technology driven world that won't slow down

Don't let this be the next Moment you miss.

Scan the QR code or visit www.theanswertrap.com to **download your free** *Map Out of the Trap* and be part of The Answer Trap movement.

I hope you'll join me.

Warmest wishes,

Kate

P.S.

If this book sparked something for you, I'd love your help spreading the word. Share your thoughts on social media, talk about it with friends or colleagues, or leave a short review on Amazon so others can discover it too. The more people who can see and name *The Answer Trap*, the better off humanity will be.

FURTHER READING AND REFERENCES

THE RIP

These sources explore how urgency, cognitive load, social pressure and perceived control drive fast action under pressure - and why our brains often reward the *feeling* of certainty over actual clarity:

- Kahneman, D. (2011). *Thinking, Fast and Slow*
  A foundational exploration of how our brain defaults to fast, automatic thinking (System 1), especially in uncertainty.

- Bazerman, M.H., & Moore, D.A. (2012). *Judgment in Managerial Decision Making*
  Examines how organisational incentives and time pressures distort decision quality and reward premature certainty.

- Dunning, D., & Kruger, J. (1999). *Unskilled and Unaware of It*
  Reveals how overconfidence arises from a lack of insight - we often feel most certain when we understand the least.

- Festinger, L. et al. (1956). *When Prophecy Fails*
  A fascinating study of belief persistence - even when confronted with contradictory evidence.

- Izuma, K. et al. (2010). *Neural correlates of cognitive dissonance*
  Shows how the brain resolves tension by reinforcing the choices we've already made - even flawed ones.

- Kruglanski, A.W., & Webster, D.M. (1996). *Motivated closing of the mind*
  Introduces the concept of 'seizing' and 'freezing' - how we grab the first plausible answer to shut down discomfort.

- Lieberman, M. D. (2013). *Social: Why Our Brains Are Wired to Connect*
  Explores how social approval and fear of appearing uncertain shape our decision-making under pressure.

- Schwartz, B. (2004). *The Paradox of Choice*
  Explains how having too many options - and needing to decide fast - can lead to shallow or avoidant choices.

- Six Seconds – 7 *Amazing facts about emotions* (https://www.6seconds.org/2022/08/19/7-amazing-facts-emotions/) – the neurochemicals that trigger emotions last for 6 seconds. It's here that The Moment begins.

THE REAL COST

These sources explore how urgency, pressure, social dynamics and emerging technologies like AI encourage fast answers - and what it takes to think beyond them:

- Baumeister, R. et al. (2011). *Decision Fatigue and Ego Depletion* – on how decision-making wears down mental capacity

- Gigerenzer, G. (2007). *Gut Feelings* – on heuristics and why our brain reaches for fast, familiar solutions

- Fast, N. J. et al. (2012). *Power and Overconfident Decision-Making* – on how certainty is rewarded over accuracy

- Lewandowsky, S. et al. (2012). *Misinformation and the Continued Influence Effect* – on why people hold onto simple, wrong ideas

- O'Neil, C. (2016). *Weapons of Math Destruction* – on how algorithmic decision-making reinforces inequality and false certainty

- Westen, D. (2007). *The Political Brain* – on how emotional appeal trumps facts in public reasoning

- Lieberman, M. D. (2013). *Social: Why Our Brains Are Wired to Connect* – on social influence and mental shortcuts

- Kashdan, T. & Rottenberg, J. (2010). *Psychological Flexibility as a Fundamental Human Strength* – on navigating ambiguity and complexity

THE AI CHALLENGE

These sources explore the potential interactions and impact of AI the human mind and cognition.

Thinking, cognition and mental effort

- David Rock – *Your Brain at Work*
  Explores how the brain handles overload, distraction and decision-making under pressure - key to understanding why the pause is so hard to protect.

- Barbara Oakley – *A Mind for Numbers*
  While focused on learning, it explains how neural pathways are built through effort, not just exposure - supports insight on 'thinking muscles'.

- Nicholas Carr – *The Shallows: What the Internet is Doing to Our Brains*
  Early but important exploration of how technology changes the way we think - not just what we think about.

Technology, AI and Prediction

- Sherry Turkle – *Reclaiming Conversation*
  A powerful investigation into how digital tools (including early AI) reshape how we connect, think and talk. She warns against 'connection without conversation' - about answers without meaning.

- Gary Marcus – *Rebooting AI*
  A critical perspective on the limits of current AI systems. He argues that AI is not intelligent in any human sense - useful for distinction between prediction and understanding.

- Ethan Mollick – *Co-Intelligence: Living and Working with AI* (2024)
  A practical guide that balances potential and pitfalls. Reinforces the message that AI should be a partner, not a proxy. Helps frame the idea of using AI as a copilot, not a driver.

- Luciano Floridi – *The Ethics of Information*
  Floridi is a leading thinker on AI ethics. He explores how meaning is shaped and lost in an age of automated information.

Institutional and organisational thinking

- Peter Senge – *The Fifth Discipline*
  Still one of the best explanations of systemic thinking and learning organisations. Connects directly to group/institutional framing.

- Matthew Syed – *Rebel Ideas*
  Explores cognitive diversity and the dangers of homogeneous thinking - support for group-level false alignment and shallow consensus.

- Edgar Schein – *Humble Inquiry*
  Encourages leaders and organisations to ask better questions rather than rush to answers. A strong cultural shift argument.

Societal impacts and cultural drift

- Neil Postman – *Amusing Ourselves to Death*
  Written about TV, but eerily relevant to AI. He warns of a culture that trades substance for performance - concern about performative thinking.

- Jonathan Haidt – *The Coddling of the American Mind*
  Focuses on how overprotection and discomfort avoidance shape public reasoning and resilience

- James Williams – *Stand Out of Our Light*
  Written by a former Google strategist turned ethicist. A sharp look at how attention is hijacked by tech, reducing our capacity for reflection.

- 'The Decline of Deep Thinking' (Scientific American) Discusses cognitive offloading and the measurable impact of digital reliance on mental effort.

- McKinsey Report: *The economic potential of generative AI* (2023) Offers practical framing of AI benefits

BEYOND THE ANSWERS

These sources explore how AI, when used thoughtfully, can extend human thinking and unlock new possibilities across various fields:

- Flynn, J. R. (1987). *Massive IQ gains in 14 nations: What IQ tests really measure.* Psychological Bulletin, 101(2), 171–191. – The original research into the Flynn Effect.

- Dutton, E., van der Linden, D., & Lynn, R. (2016). *The Negative Flynn Effect: A systematic literature review.* Intelligence, 59, 163–169 – A study showing how traditional intelligence is in reverse.

- Barzilay, R., & Collins, J. (2020). *Artificial intelligence yields new antibiotic* – on how AI identified halicin, a novel antibiotic effective against resistant bacteria.

- Re-thinking The Future (n.d.). *The Use of Generative AI in the Architectural Industry* – on how AI assists architects in designing energy-efficient and sustainable buildings.

- Space.com (2021). *AI discovers over 300 unknown exoplan-ets in Kepler telescope data* – on how AI algorithms uncovered previously undetected exoplanets.

- Ultralytics (2024). *Harnessing AI to Combat Deforestation* –on how AI-powered systems analyze satellite imagery to detect deforestation activities. Link

- AI Novelist (n.d.). *AI Novelist   2.0* – on how Japanese authors use AI tools to explore different writing styles and narratives.

HOW WE THINK

These sources explore how motivation, disruption and cognitive patterns shape everyday action - and what happens when thinking can't keep up:

- Christensen, C. M. (2005). *Jobs to be Done theory* – on how people act to make progress, not just complete tasks
- Heath, C. & Heath, D. (2010). *Switch: How to Change Things When Change Is Hard* – on how to create better mental pathways when the usual ones fail
- Baumeister, R. & Tierney, J. (2011). *Willpower* – on how mental energy depletes under cognitive load and emotional stress
- Gollwitzer, P. M. (1999). *Implementation intentions* – on how small cognitive shortcuts can help bridge the gap between motivation and action

THE AUTOPILOTS

- Sternberg, R. J. (1997). *Successful Intelligence* – on how adaptive thinking draws on analytical, creative and practical intelligence to navigate everyday life

These sources explore how urgency, cognitive load and perceived control drive fast action under pressure:

- Sweller, J. (1988). *Cognitive Load Theory* – on mental shortcuts under stress

- Darley, J. M., & Batson, C. D. (1973). *'From Jerusalem to Jericho'* – on how time pressure impacts moral action

- Baumeister, R. F. et al. (1998). *Ego Depletion and Decision Fatigue* – on what happens when decision-making resources get worn down

Explore the science behind our need for certainty, the risks of overthinking and the limits of information:

- Nickerson, R. S. (1998). *Confirmation Bias* – on how we seek data that supports our beliefs

- Hsu, M. et al. (2005). *Neural responses to uncertainty* – showing how the brain reacts to unknown outcomes

- Blanchard, T. C. et al. (2016). *Uncertainty and pain* – on the emotional cost of waiting and indecision

Dive into the research behind exploration, autonomy and creative reframing under pressure:

- Deci, E. & Ryan, R. (1985). *Self-Determination Theory* – on autonomy, mastery and intrinsic motivation

- Kashdan, T. B. & Rottenberg, J. (2010). *Psychological flexibility as a fundamental human strength* – on adaptability and openness

- Gopnik, A. (2009). *The Scientist in the Crib* – early research on exploratory learning and curiosity

- Grant, A. (2021). *Think Again* – on the power of rethinking and intellectual humility

These works explore how humans seek shared meaning, emotional coherence and relational safety when complexity hits:

- Weick, K. (1995). *Sensemaking in Organizations* – on how people restore meaning in volatile situations

- Sorce, J. F. et al. (1985). *Emotional referencing in infants* – on how humans use social cues to make sense of ambiguity

- Lieberman, M.D. (2013). *Social: Why Our Brains Are Wired to Connect* – on the neuroscience of human connection and meaning-making

- Bowlby, J. (1969). *Attachment Theory* – on how connection is a biological drive in moments of threat

These sources explore perfectionism, the cognitive urge to refine under pressure and how overfocus can stall action:

- Frost, R. O. et al. (1990). *Dimensions of Perfectionism* – foundational work on the motivations behind perfectionist behaviour

- Egan, S. J. et al. (2011). *Perfectionism as a transdiagnostic process* – exploring the emotional function of refinement

- Baumeister, R. F. (1998). *The self and the control of behavior* – on the link between control, performance and fear of failure

- Schwartz, B. (2004). *The Paradox of Choice* – on how more options (and more refinement) can lead to paralysis

THE VITAL THREAD

- Christiansen, K. (2016). *The Thrive Cycle: How to build an unstoppable, customer-driven organisation by activating its adaptive DNA.* – Chapter 9 – The Vital Thread. A detailed description of what it is, why it works and how to create one.

www.ingramcontent.com/pod-product-compliance
Lightning Source LLC
Chambersburg PA
CBHW031117020426
42333CB00012B/122